D0340068

To Helen:

For

every rich grace

Walter J. Burghardt, S.J.

Sept. 1983

SEASONS
THAT LAUGH OR WEEP

also by Walter J. Burghardt, S.J.
published by Paulist Press

TELL THE NEXT GENERATION
SIR, WE WOULD LIKE TO SEE JESUS

SEASONS
THAT LAUGH OR WEEP

Musings on the Human Journey

WALTER J. BURGHARDT, S.J.
Theologian in Residence
Georgetown University

Paulist Press • New York/Ramsey

"To Torey With Much 'Love' " from ONE CHILD
by Torey L. Hayden is reprinted with permission
of G.P. Putnam's Sons, copyright © 1980.

An excerpt from John Gruen's article "The Saint—
An Opera That Mirrors Menotti's Soul"
from April 16, 1978 (Arts & Leisure) © 1978
is reprinted by permission of The New York Times.

An excerpt from "Meditations on the Church"
by Henri de Lubac, S.J., is taken from
VATICAN II: AN INTERFAITH APPRAISAL, ed. John H. Miller, C.S.C.,
copyright © 1966 by University of Notre Dame Press,
Notre Dame, Indiana and Association Press,
New York, New York.

Copyright © 1983 by
Walter J. Burghardt, S.J.

All rights reserved. No part of this book may be reproduced
or transmitted in any form or by any means, electronic or mechanical,
including photocopying, recording, or by any information storage and
retrieval system without permission in writing from the Publisher.

Library of Congress Catalog Card Number: 83-60655

ISBN: 0-8091-0347-8

Published by Paulist Press
545 Island Road, Ramsey, N.J. 07446

Printed and bound in the United States of America

TABLE OF CONTENTS

for MARY ANN *and* PIERCE

---

whose memories season my own

"Thou art more
than the day or the morrow,
the seasons that laugh or that weep."

Algernon Charles Swinburne
Hymn to Proserpine

PRELUDE

Six years ago I was worried. I found myself . . . remembering. And that, they tell me, is a disease of the graying and the balding. To go back is to bore, to praise "the good old days." To remember is to bask in the past, to enter an Eden that never existed, a paradise as legendary as Atlantis. To remember is to start dying.

But then I began to see: no, 'tis not so; quite the opposite. It began for me with Israel. I recalled Rabbi Abraham Joshua Heschel's startling affirmation: much of what the Bible demands can be summed up in a single word—remember! I discovered in ancient Israel a community of faith vitalized by memory, a people that knew God by reflecting not on the mysteries of nature but on its own history. To actualize was to retain within time and space the memory and the mystery of God's saving presence. And Elie Wiesel, that remarkable Jewish storyteller who feels guilty because he survived the Holocaust, has reminded us that, for Jews, to forget is a crime against justice *and* memory: if you forget, you become the executioner's accomplice.

I moved out from Israel. I recovered a 1959 editorial in *Life:* "Anyone who wants to know who he is should start by finding out where he came from and where he's been." Harvard's systematic theologian Gordon Kaufman pointed out that the events of any historical process become history through human memory; the past is always alive and active in the present.

Perhaps most importantly, Johannes Metz distinguished our memories. There are memories that simply make us feel good, because they glide over all that is oppressive and demanding. And there are memories that are dangerous, because they make demands on us, reveal perilous insights for today, illuminate harshly the questionable nature of things with which we have come to terms. For the Christian, I recalled, the most demanding type of memory is memory of the passion, death, and resurrection of Jesus Christ. For, as Henri Nouwen expressed it in a work provocatively titled *The Living Reminder,* "By connecting the human story with the story of the suffering servant, we rescue our history from its fatalistic chain and allow our time to be converted from *chronos* into *kairos,* from a series of randomly organized incidents and accidents into a constant opportunity to explore God's works in our lives."

To remember, then, is to start . . . living. This brief book has a profound presupposition. If we are to find our way through our future, we must find our way through our past. This book, then, is a memory—better still, a memorializing. That hazardous "I" is inescapable here; but, aware that the best of Burghardt is not necessarily the cream of Catholicism, I shall paint on a broader canvas, a canvas that borrows liberally from others, a canvas that may provoke your own memories.

As a framework for remembering, I am making free use of Daniel J. Levinson's *The Seasons of a Man's Life*. The term "life cycle," this study tells us, has two especially crucial meanings. The first is process or journey: the movement from birth to old age follows a universal pattern, a basic sequence. The second is seasons: the life cycle, the journey, the process is not a simple, continuous, unchanging flow. Like a year or a day, like love and war and politics, like illness and artistic creation, each season is different, has its distinctive character, links past and future, contains past and future within itself.

How divide and describe these seasons? Levinson's research isolates four seasons: (1) childhood and adolescence, 0 to 17, then a five-year transition, a zone of overlap; (2) early adulthood, 22 to 40, then a five-year transition; (3) middle adulthood, 45 to 60, then a five-year transition; (4) late adulthood, 65 and beyond.

Understandably, but unfortunately for us, Levinson's research is restricted to the male. Women, he believes, "go through the same adult developmental periods as men ... but in partially different ways that reflect the differences in biology and social circumstances." Levinson's approach "offers a basis for the study of women, without the assumption that the two genders develop in either identical or totally different ways."

Those concerned to discover more explicitly the developmental rhythms of women would profit from Gail Sheehy's *Passages* and Anita Spencer's *Seasons*. And, of course, our understanding of psychological and moral development can be deepened immeasurably if we plumb the research of Erik Erikson, Jean Piaget, and Lawrence Kohlberg. For my purposes, however, rigid brackets of age and evolution, of personality and crisis, are not imperative. Sufficient that the seasons are there, that we can describe them with fair accuracy, that the experience of others can be helpful—to a point. In the last analysis, *I* am my seasons. It is our own story each of us must tell.

Those who know me as an academic person, with both feet firmly planted in the first six or seven centuries, may raise eyebrows when they meet this slender volume. How came he to this? Superficially, it began in 1978, when I was asked to deliver the keynote address at the Seventh Annual Conference sponsored by the University of Notre Dame's Center for Pastoral Liturgy. The conference theme was provocative: "Human Journeys, Liturgical Journeys." Its overarching thesis was that the liturgy ritualizes, symbolizes, sacramentalizes what goes on in the rest of our lives. To liturgical prayer we bring our daily experience. It was my task to illustrate the human journey, leaving to liturgiologists the more difficult burden of revealing how human journeys become liturgical journeys, how the memorializing of Jesus' passion, death, and resurrection connects your story and mine with the story of the Suffering Servant.

When the Indiana dust had settled, Robert Heyer of the Paulist Press suggested that I expand the original paper into a modest paperback. We agreed that the way to go would be to enrich my profoundly personal memories with the experiences of others, especially as these emerge from literature, from biography, from the fine arts. Not a technical tome, not a scholarly study; rather, very human reflections that might speak to "ordinary people," stimulate their own remembering, perhaps persuade some one man or woman whose winter is discontent to start . . . living.

In point of fact, this book was germinating within me even before fellow Jesuit John Gallen lured me to Notre Dame. So much of this I have wanted to say for ever so long, have said fragmentarily in homilies and addresses but have never put together. Why in a book? You might understand if I reproduce a paragraph from Richard Bach's *Illusions: The Adventures of a Reluctant Messiah*. Towards the close of this delightful, insightful allegory, the "messiah from Indiana" is puzzled by the reluctance of Richard ("one messiah in a world of others") to put his convictions and his experiences on paper:

> Maybe I'm just dumb, Richard, and maybe I don't see something obvious that you see very well, and if I don't see it will you please tell me, but what is wrong with writing it down on paper? Is there a rule that a messiah can't write what he thinks is true, the things that have been fun for him, that work for him? And then maybe if people don't like what he says, instead of shooting him they can burn his words, hit the ashes with a stick? And if they do like it, they can read the words another time, or write them on a refrigerator door, or play with whatever ideas make sense to them? Is there something wrong with writing? But maybe I'm just dumb.

More pertinent still is a sentence from Bach's preface. Although he does not enjoy writing (I do), "once in a while there's a great dynamite-burst of flying glass and brick and splinters through the front wall and somebody stalks over the rubble, seizes me by the throat and gently says: 'I will not let you go until you set me, in words, on paper.'"

Across the rubble of the years, someone—good Spirit or mischievous elf, I know not—has me by the throat and will not let go. If the result is a thought you can scotch-tape to your refrigerator door, I shall be delighted.

Walter J. Burghardt, S.J.
Georgetown University
January 21, 1983

SPRING

The first of human seasons (birth to 17) is the prelude to adulthood. It is life's springtime. A family or an equivalent social unit provides protection, socialization, support of growth. The infant evolves into a separate person, learns to distinguish the me from the not-me. The child expands his or her social world to a school, to a wider peer group, to a neighborhood, begins to resolve emotional struggles. Bodily changes move the child to adolescence; other changes, of flesh and spirit, lead gradually to adulthood.

VULNERABLE

Springtime's child is dreadfully immature and frightfully vulnerable. Immature, in part, because my experience is so limited, and yet it is all the experience I have, all I know, all I

11

can realistically live by. Vulnerable because defenseless before
so much that shapes me, from the flesh impressed on me without my say-so to the word incautiously mouthed within my
hearing.

In this context I resonate feelingly to an experience of that
remarkable French writer Simone Weil (1909–43). At 14 she
passed through her darkest spiritual crisis. It was, she remarked in her spiritual autobiography, "one of those fits of bot-
tomless despair that come with adolescence." What caused it?
A keen sense of her utter unworthiness, intensified by agonizing migraine headaches. These headaches, rarely absent, she
came to see later as a special gift. In early adolescence, however, they were only the outward sign of her inner misery—a
profound conviction that she was totally lacking in talent. Her
brother was a mathematical prodigy, and she never forgot a remark she overheard from a visitor to her mother: the boy "is
genius itself"; the girl is "beauty." And so, forever after, this
singularly gifted woman did her best to hide or destroy what
was superficially charming in her, what was beautiful. Through
shapeless dress, clumsy gestures, unmusical voice she put to
death sheer beauty. Nor did she ever abandon an abysmal
sense of her own stupidity.

Yes, to be young is to be vulnerable. It is the poet Robert
Lowell cruelly kidded by classmates ("Dimbulb," "Droopy-
drawers") and carrying the scars for life:

> I was fifteen;
> they made me cry in public.

To be young is to be confused and confusing. In the moving screenplay *The 400 Blows,* François Truffaut chronicles his
own adolescence, his experience that adolescence is painful, is
marked not only by the onset of puberty but by an inferiority
complex and a yearning for independence, that any simple up-

set can spark the crisis we call adolescent rebellion: "the world is unjust, one must cope with it anyway, and one way to cope is to raise hell."

And so we see 13-year-old Antoine Doinel at once terrified and rather proud of a mother who conceived him out of wedlock, wanted to abort him, doesn't really like him very much, is always bawling him out "for nothing . . . for little things." His father is "all right, I guess. But he's a bit of a coward because he knows my mother's unfaithful, but he says nothing so that there won't be any fights at home."

Servile to his parents, Antoine is arrogant and sarcastic to others. A mouse at home, he rattles a mile a minute outside. At 13 he is already cynical, unscrupulous, sneaky. He is always late. He steals—even tries to pawn his father's typewriter. He is a mixture of bad conduct and good: he will haul the coal from the cellar but then wipes his black hands on the curtain. He is touchingly devilish: meeting a priest in a long black robe, he hails him "Bonjour, madame!" His best friend is an adolescent so different that he complements Antoine very well—less aggressive but far more independent, more resourceful, more relaxed, more Machiavellian.

Antoine works out of one troublesome situation only to fall into another, and so he is constantly ridden by anxiety. He runs away because he cannot face the anger at home, is sent to a center for juvenile delinquents because his father can no longer endure him, doesn't want to take him back. "Do whatever you want with him; take him away, put him in the country somewhere. Who knows, it might do him some good. We can't figure him out. He needs some real punishment. . . ."

As I look back upon adolescence over the bridge of a half century, I find that John Steinbeck's *The Red Pony* gives vivid expression to several teen-age experiences and discoveries. You may remember ten-year-old Jody Tiflin, shy, polite, unquestioningly obedient to a disciplinarian father who despises weakness, sickness, helplessness. He lives for Thanksgiving, when he can ride the red pony bought for him at auction. But the rains come, and the pony takes cold. His legs tremble with ague; each breath is a groan; a hole is cut in his windpipe, to no avail; he escapes to a little clearing in the brush, where the buzzards circle around till he dies. And Jody despairingly beats one buzzard to the ground, strikes it again and again with a piece of white quartz till its head is a red pulp, and Jody has to be pulled off with force.

And you may remember how Jody waits and works eight months for the mare Nellie to throw her colt; but when the time comes, the colt is "turned all around wrong," and Jody must watch Billy Buck knock Nellie unconscious with a horse-shoe hammer, rip open the tough belly with a pocketknife, force out a little black head, little slick, wet ears. "For a moment he held the little black colt in his arms and looked at it. And then he walked slowly over and laid it in the straw at Jody's feet. 'There's your colt. I promised. And there it is. I had to do it—had to.' "

The lessons of adolescence? One perspective Steinbeck connoisseur has summed it up in a pithy sentence: "a statement of certain truths [Steinbeck] had always felt in his bones—that there is no fulfillment without sacrifice, that fulfillment and frustration go hand in hand, and that, even though it would be pleasant to believe it, there is no natural law which assures Man of a reward fitly matched to his endeavor."

The adolescent virtue, Erik Erikson insists, is fidelity. He defines this as "the ability to sustain loyalties freely pledged in spite of the inevitable contradictions of value systems." How does fidelity reveal itself in youth? In a high sense of duty, in truthfulness, in genuineness, in loyalty, in fairness, in "all that is implied in devotion—a freely given but binding vow, with the fateful implication of a curse befalling traitors." Such fideli-

ty "is the cornerstone of identity." Nevertheless, it is not realized in a context of self-sufficient adolescent independence; it
calls for "confirming adults and affirming peers."

The loyalty and devotion of which Erikson writes I find
touchingly in the boy Manolin in Ernest Hemingway's last major work, *The Old Man and the Sea.* "The old man had taught
the boy to fish and the boy loved him." It saddens Manolin to
see Santiago come in each day with his skiff empty. "Everything about him was old except his eyes and they were the
same color as the sea and were cheerful and undefeated."
Manolin no longer fishes with him, not because he doubts the
old man but because he must obey his father. Unlike many of
the fishermen, the boy never laughs at the old man. "If I cannot fish with you, I would like to serve in some way." He goes
along with Santiago's fictions, talks seriously with him about
"the baseball" and "the great DiMaggio," covers his shoulders
with an old army blanket, brings him stew and beer. "There
are many good fishermen and some great ones. But there is
only you." And when the old man returns half-dead with only
the skeleton of the shark-eaten eighteen-foot marlin and falls
asleep in his shack, Manolin comes in, sees that he is breathing,
then sees the old man's battered hands and starts to cry. He
goes out quietly to bring some coffee and all the way down the
road he is crying. And he tells Santiago that, despite his family,
he will fish with him again, "for I still have much to learn." As
the story ends, the old man is sleeping once more on his face
and the boy is sitting by him watching him.

CHRIST'S CHILD

Simone and Robert, Antoine and Jody and Manolin, each
speaks tellingly to an adolescence I can to some extent dredge
out of my youth but much more vividly have experienced all

around me through half a century. And yet, in all these narratives something is not touched which only a profound faith can supply.

In the Christian vision, the human journey begins before birth. You see, you and I came into this world deprived. Rich or poor, we were disadvantaged. Coloring each conception was Sin with a capital S. Theologians of sin disagree in diagnosing this "Sin of the world." When *I* first bore its weight, it seemed simple enough. I was a fallen god. In a distant Paradise there had been a prehistoric catastrophe. The first man, at the peak of human powers, rebelled in cold blood against his Creator. In punishment, he lost God, self-mastery, endless life— not only for himself and wife Eve, but for all who would be seeded from him. And so I came whimpering into the world deprived of God's presence, guilty because I shared mysteriously in Adam's no, unable to recapture a Paradise lost, enslaved to passion, destined for a life in which, like St. Paul, "I can will what is right, but I cannot do it" (Rom 7:18).

Not quite, say recent researchers into sin; the myth must be reinterpreted; the perspective has to be evolutionary; the center has to be Christ. My status at birth was not a solidarity in sin with a historic Adam; it was the human condition: I was not-yet-in-Christ. And I was not-yet-in-Christ because I was situated in a sinful world, in a world constituted by the whole history of sinful deeds from the first to the latest. The "Sin of the world" became my sin because my very existence is constituted by my relations with others; this situation is not external to me, it is intrinsic to me. And paradoxically, the good news of the superabundance of grace is that this sinful world is not "without Christ," save where a human heart freely closes itself to Christ.

The reinterpretations are many and complex; this is not the place to evaluate them. But perhaps a paragraph from theologian Piet Smulders' *The Design of Teilhard de Chardin* describes our natal condition in a way most reflective Christians can accept:

> In the heart of man lies a kind of will not to love God; anterior to every personal choice, it encompasses and fetters that choice. Created and destined to love, man always aspires, at least unconsciously, to love as the final flowering and ultimate fulfillment of his being; but he has set up a deep-cutting egotism in the innermost chamber of himself. He suffers from a "curvitas," a deviation that turns back upon finite goods and chiefly upon himself.... In this way, original sin might perhaps be described as a deep-seated bias within the very existence of each person, a bias stemming from the very fact that the individual has been born into the human family....

I invaded this world with a prepersonal bias prior to any act of mine, a prepersonal unwillingness to grow in the likeness of Christ, an involuntary aversion from God and connivance with the sins of others, a prevoluntary rejection of God's love, an inclination to evil prior to choice. I invaded this world calling mutely, from the depths of my being, for Christ's liberating action. I needed a conversion at a level deeper than the voluntary.

Precisely here, as I see it now, was the underlying significance of my baptism. It was not only entrance into a believing community; it was the first stage in a process, a journey, of conversion. God's grace was touching the involuntary at the heart of my freedom; God was beginning to remove the bias toward evil, the deep-seated desire to be held captive, the unconscious connivance with sin at the root of my being. It was unimportant that I *felt* only cold water and not warm grace; God was at work in the depths of my person, preparing the way for a free, personal, total turning to Him in full awareness of His liberating presence. He *was* there.

Childhood and adolescence should be a Christian spring, a

coming to awareness: awareness of God and awareness of sin. I like to think that my awareness of God came first; I am sure that my awareness of sin soon became the more powerful. Catalogue of sins, examination of conscience, confession—God was indeed there, but taken for granted; sin was more pervasive, more pressing. Not that I sinned boldly or passionately or convincingly; I did not. Nothing like sixteen-year-old Augustine, whose "one delight was to love and be loved," who "could not distinguish the white light of love from the fog of lust. Both love and lust boiled within me, and swept my youthful immaturity over the precipice of evil desires to leave me half drowned in a whirlpool of abominable sins." His mother kept urging him "not to sin with women, above all not with any man's wife." In his immaturity he did not realize that God was speaking through her. "All this sounded to me womanish and I should have blushed to obey."

Nor can I remember, like Augustine and his stolen pears, sinning for the sake of sinning, sin sweetened by the sheer sinning:

> . . . I chose to steal, and not because want drove me to it. . . .
> For I stole things which I already had in plenty and of better
> quality. Nor had I any desire to enjoy the things I stole, but
> only the stealing of them and the sin. There was a pear tree
> near our vineyard, heavy with fruit, but fruit that was not
> particularly tempting either to look at or to taste. A group of
> young blackguards, and I among them, went out to knock
> down the pears and carry them off late one night. . . . We car-
> ried off an immense load of pears, not to eat—for we barely
> tasted them before throwing them to the hogs. Our only
> pleasure in doing it was that it was forbidden. . . . [I had] no
> cause for wrongdoing save my wrongness. The malice of the
> act was base and I loved it—that is to say I loved my own un-
> doing. I loved the evil in me—not the thing for which I did
> the evil, simply the evil. . . .

No, I did not roar with the Roaring Twenties. But even in my love for God there was more piety than passion. Why? Behind it, I suspect, was our Anglo-Saxon legacy: passion is something to be ashamed of. For strong feeling is a sign of weakness; the manly reaction to reality is stoicism. Love, of course, but let not love enrapture you, let it not glow. Be afraid, if you must, but keep your teeth from chattering. Take joy from a sonata, but let it not thrill you. Death will always sadden, but you dare not weep (weeping is for women). Detest sin, but never be distressed by it. Protest injustice, but grow not black with anger. Feelings were dangerous; only cold reason could be trusted.

And still there was an incipient experience of God. No sudden, startling, breath-taking conversion here. But a conversion all the same—a gradual, almost inexorable turning to God. It stemmed in large measure from exposure. I mean exposure to parents with old-fashioned immigrant virtues: tough, honest, loyal, just. A mother and father with little education, hard workers with hands and heart, living before my eyes and infusing into my bloodstream what Christian existence should be: to live for others. This was their life: my brother and I. *We* were their life—their joy and their sorrow.

My father had a strong sense of justice. He never learned its formal definition; he simply assumed that if you were supposed to do something, or had said you would, you did it. No excuses. He himself worked a tough milk-wagon route from 3 a.m. to 3 p.m. six days a week—with rare vacation and no sick leave, even when the horse split his chin open with a vicious kick. Justice was this shy man's way of saying three difficult words: "I love you."

I remember—I might have been four or five—my mother taking me to the park. For some reason I broke away from her, raced along the stony path, tripped, bruised a knee badly.

Mother knew from experience what would happen when the head of the house returned from milk delivery. Anxiously she cleaned me up as best she could, but the short pants of the day left little room for secrecy. The conversation was brief and to the point. "What happened to him?" "Well, he fell." "But weren't you holding his hand?" "Yes, but he ran away." "How could he run away? Weren't you holding his hand?"

It had good effects on me: devotion to duty, sensitivity to the pledged word. Still, like so much excess of virtue, it made for problems that would surface only later: a certain rigidity, intolerance of imperfection, even some unhealthy guilt.

Part of my experience of God was exposure to a remarkable group of priests, five diocesan priests who staffed the parish of St. John the Evangelist on New York City's East 55th Street as I grew up. One especially, Francis X. Shea, used to stop me every so often. I can still see him, black hat under his arm, priestly in poise and still so attractively human, just chatting with a boy on the block, but often asking: "What are you going to be?" And after a while: "Do you still want to be a priest?" Actually, I never wanted to be anything else. Not even a fireman or a cowboy.

Highly influential was my exposure to a parochial school with its unvarying pattern of prayers, crucifix, religious instruction—and black habits. Happily, I cannot blame any nuns for my psychological twists or guilt feelings. These Sisters of Charity were rather like the nuns in novelist Mary McCarthy's *Memories of a Catholic Girlhood,* for they taught me "a religion of beauty and goodness, however imperfectly realized." I have an uneasy feeling, however, that in those days I must have provided a fair imitation of Landor's "clever, upright little prig."

Those no-nonsense nuns led me to a Jesuit high school, semimilitary, with a major stress on discipline: disciplined intelligence, disciplined emotions, disciplined body, disciplined will. I can still hear the prefect of discipline, a World War I chaplain, bellowing like a top sergeant: "Son, there's no excuse for being late!" "But, Father, suppose there's an accident in the subway?" "Son, if you're killed in that accident, your dead body's got to be here by 9!" It could be rough, and only the masochists reveled in it, but the educational philosophy was clear: you are not fit to lead if you have not first learned to obey—and, as at home, without questioning. Regular confession, regular Mass, regular Communion. It made for an atmosphere perhaps not "charged with the grandeur of God," but where God could be recognized. Not felt . . . recognized.

Not so obvious but hardly less important was ceaseless exposure to God's multiform presence, the reflection of His glory in the works of His hands: a whirlwind reflecting His power, a mountain mirroring His majesty, surging waves His irresistibleness, a star-flecked sky His breath-taking loveliness. Even seeing, with Joseph Mary Plunkett, Jesus' "blood upon the rose/ and in the stars the glory of his eyes,/ His body gleams amid eternal snows,/ His tears fall from the skies." Encounter? Not a meeting face to face; not a mystical experience. More like a hazy, lazy June day. If the God of my baptism touched me at the level of the unconscious, the God of my adolescence touched me at the conscious level, the level of choice, of freedom; but still that awareness was not awfully reflective.

TODAY'S CHILD

Now *my* adolescence is not programmatic for today. World War II and TV, the human cry for freedom and man's first steps on the moon—these have fashioned a new world. In the 60's the historian Thomas Berry uncovered three characteristics of this world that differentiate it radically from the old. First, its universality: there simply are no isolated islands—

whether nations or cultures or continents. The thoughts and problems of one person are now the thoughts and problems of the entire world; the creative work of one segment of the world is shared almost instantly by all. Second, this new world is not fixed, not static; it is developmental, dynamic. The reality of structures is change. Third, humanism: contemporary men and women center not on some cosmic order, not on God, but on man, on the human person.

In this new world, boys and girls grow up more rapidly than I did. Home and church, school and society—these make not for security but for problems. More conflict with parent and president, with pastor and pope. Earlier experience of evil, more profound experience. Drugs, sex, blood—all part of the air they breathe, the music they sway to, the tube they glue to. God is not a blanket; God is a problem. A hell to come is not what many adolescents fear; for many, hell is here.

In some parts of the world countless boys and girls do not grow up at all. I cannot forget a 1979 Associated Press photograph: a Cambodian mother cradling the rigid body of her dead child—today's Pietà, reproduced time without number. In four years four million Cambodians had died—half the nation, most of them children. Each day, as *Time* described it, a hundred or a thousand Cambodians were stumbling into Thailand "on reed-thin legs . . . a grisly cavalcade of specters, wrapped in black rags. Many are in the last stages of malnutrition, or are ravaged by . . . dysentery, tuberculosis and malaria. Perhaps the most pathetic images of all are those of tearful, exhausted mothers cradling hollow-eyed children with death's-head faces, their bellies swollen, their limbs as thin and fragile as dried twigs." No, my adolescence is hardly programmatic for today.

As for those who do grow up, I find fascinating religious differences from the adolescent I knew, the adolescent I was, a half century ago. The temptation of the Geritol generation is to see the New Breed of the 80's as irresponsible and undisciplined, uncommitted and uncaring, heedless of God and skeptical of church, devoid of doctrine and devotion. There are indeed such adolescents, but the indictment is far too sweeping. The change in religious consciousness that the sociologist Andrew Greeley has discovered among Catholic teen-agers, a transformation he believes is the result of reforms instituted by the Second Vatican Council, will startle the pessimist and delight the optimist. Greeley's own summary statement deserves to be quoted exactly:

> The New Breed of the 1980's is more likely to think of God as a mother and a lover, and of heaven as a life of action and pleasure. Its story of its love affair with God, and thus the meaning of its life, represents a dramatic change in Catholic religious sensibility, a change apparently caused by Vatican Council II and transmitted by devout mothers, sympathetic parish priests and passionately loving spouses. Because of this new vision of God and of life, the New Breed is more likely to be open to church careers, more socially committed, more insistent on high quality church performance by the church, more formal in their prayer, more concerned about racial justice, and more personally devout (but not more committed to the church's sexual teaching or to infallibility . . .). Their personal devotion may sag during the alienation interlude in the middle-20's, but the rest of their new religious sensibility is likely to remain unaltered.

Thus does empirical data bolster my superficial experience. It does not deny youth's vulnerability, its confusions, its rebellions. It simply corrects our myopia. It assures us that there is more substance and depth to today's adolescent than meets the aging eye.

Perceptive religious educators such as the Jesuit James Di-Giacomo confirm Greeley's conclusions. They find our young people seeking God in impressive numbers and with an urgency rare a decade ago. Many are weary of freedom without direction, suspect self-indulgence without commitment. If they resist our adult religions, it is because "they don't want to be part of something that looks narrow, uninspiring, cramping, dying or dead. They ascribe this bad scene to the Policeman God of a rule-keeping church taught by moralistic teachers and managed by greedy clerics who preside over dull liturgies."

This young breed of the 80's poses provocative challenges to Christian parents and educators. How relate their yearning for a warm, friendly Lover God, where Abba = Daddy, to the all-holy, sovereign Creator Lord who transcends all our human imaginings? How help them see that real love is "more than a rub and a tickle," that love makes demands, discipleship costs, leads to a cross? How persuade them that, if Mass is tedious repetition, so too is much that is crucial to human living—education, scientific research, coronary bypasses, even the meals for which "we keep showing up, three times a day, with remarkable fidelity"? It has to be done; for with them lies our hope for church and world. It can be done; for their idealism needs only to be set afire, and God's grace knows no limits save our selfishness.

Let me tell you about young Sean Acker. Age 12 as I write, he is all boy, similar to others but not the same. Tall, left of hand and big of feet, he usually imprisons his unruly brown hair in a baseball cap. He plays soccer and the violin, races from skate board to fish pole, loves classical music and likes rock. A quiet lad, he devours books the way he gorges spaghetti with garlic bread: both transport him into another world. He is gentle and sensitive, responsive to others' needs, and so he makes friends easily but has trouble at times with the pressures of his peers. He revels in fantasy, is sentimental over animals, hugs his mother (but why must mothers forever "explain"?). When he gets angry, he lowers his head, hunches his shoulders, sticks out his elbows, and stomps like a skinny Walter Matthau. Here are just two products (unedited) of his teeming imagination—one a serious little gem, the other characteristically playful:

OCEAN

Dangerous, yet curious,
Proceeding and receding.
The struggle of life occurring within.

THE PERPENDICULAR PRICKLE

This is a Perpendicular Prickle.
Perpendicular Prickles live in Panamanian pastures in pretty deep
   pits far past perfect.

Perpendicular Prickles eat partridges from Peru, but are partial
   to parsley. They also eat pastrami with pickles.

Perpendicular Prickles enjoy parties in Pasadena, but picking at
   pumpkin papers is their pastime. They like to pretend
   they're the Prime Minister while flying over the Prime Meridian.

Perpendicular Prickles perch on pentagons and pose for people.
   They paint priceless pictures of peaches using only primary
   colors. They pinch pre-school principals precisely on the
   posterior.

This Perpendicular Prickle perspires, which made puddles on my
   poem.

Now Sean is fortunate. The air he breathes is compounded of intelligence and love, of humor and understanding. It doesn't make him invulnerable, doesn't guarantee that his teens will be a round-the-clock Disneyland inhabited by all manner of Perpendicular Prickles. It does promise a web of relationships, a sort of supporting cast—parents and relatives, teachers and friends—that makes it possible to move through adolescence naturally, with little worse than the usual run of teen-age aches.

But uncounted thousands of Sean's brothers and sisters cannot count on such supports, and so their experience of spring is far more tempestuous—or, what may be crueler still, deadly unexciting. Even in America. Some are "latchkey children": after school they let themselves into an empty house. Some have never tasted love—never. Some cannot read, and so a whole magical world is hidden from their eyes. Some go to bed hungry or suffer from malnutrition. You know, there are North American babies, like West African babies, who are too weak to do more than whimper, whose minds and bodies are already beyond repair. I shall never forget how Arthur Simon once pictured the human family:

> Imagine ten children at a table dividing up food. The three healthiest load their plates with large portions, including most of the meat, fish, milk and eggs. They eat what they want and discard the leftovers. Two other children get just enough to meet their basic requirements. The remaining five are left wanting. Three of them—sickly, nervous, apathetic children—manage to stave off the feeling of hunger by filling up on bread and rice. The other two cannot do even that. One dies from dysentery and the second from pneumonia, which they are too weak to ward off. These children represent the human family. . . .

And these children represent the world's children.

Paradoxically, the answer is not affluence. A 20-mile stretch of lakefront along Chicago's North Shore, one of the nation's richest areas, is known among local therapists as "the suicide belt." In a 17-month period, 28 teen-agers took their own lives: 18 by gunshot, 8 by hanging, 2 by lying down in front of trains. With affluent youngsters elsewhere, they fit, in disproportionate numbers, into some grisly statistics: suicide is the third leading cause of death among Americans 15 to 19, close behind accidents and homicides.

Why? In and around Chicago the responses are varied. Teen-agers complain that their parents hand them everything on a silver platter—everything save love, understanding, acceptance as persons. Counselors and therapists argue that parents expect too much in return for abundance, refuse to see their children as average, make the underachievers feel like failures. Some experts lay the blame on an unreal TV: real problems are solved in half an hour. Others point to the breakdown of the extended family, a narcissistic culture, post-Viet Nam disillusionment with government, family, all institutions. The poor share their misery, act out frustration in antisocial ways; the affluent, forced to be competitive, feel ever more alone, take it out not on society but on themselves. Finally, you have the sad commentary of a Los Angeles psychiatrist: "There's nothing to distract a teen-ager today."

This is not to say that the average teen-ager is unhappy. In fact, a recent survey of *The Adolescent: A Psychological Self-Portrait* concludes that 85% of normal American teen-agers feel happy most of the time. Still, happiness is not quite what it was in the early 60's. Then youngsters were more confident, more trusting, felt greater affection for their families, were more in control of "their inner feelings and impulses." In the late 70's and in 1980, teen-agers' self-image was "decidedly less positive." They were less secure, worried more about their bodies, were more easily hurt, had lower ethical standards.

Why? No single answer seems to satisfy; several factors may have conspired: Viet Nam, Watergate, the economy, the divorce rate. Whatever the causes, they make for statistics that alarm me: one out of every five teen-agers is empty emotionally, is confused much of the time, would rather die than go on living.

Let me end our springtime on a more encouraging note. I

have just finished Torey Hayden's stirring true story *One Child*. Hayden taught "young human refuse," the disadvantaged no one else could or would teach. Into her class of eight comes Sheila, a tiny, hostile, smelly six-year-old who tied a boy of three to a tree and burned him critically. She lives in a migrant camp with a father who calls her a bastard without a decent bone in her body. Most of her early years he has spent in prison and in a state hospital for alcoholism and drug dependency. Her mother, 14 when Sheila was born, deserted her two years before; she simply pushed Sheila out of a car and left her at the roadside. At home Sheila rarely talks, never weeps. "I don't never cry." Why not? "Ain't nobody can hurt me that ways. They don't know I hurt if I don't cry."

In Hayden's class Sheila proves a problem. Though her IQ is phenomenal, off the page, she does not want to learn; she refuses to be touched, to be helped, to be liked. She is destructive, pokes out the eyes of goldfish with a pencil. She trusts no one, is wary and easily frightened, screeches long and loud in rage. A touching combination of vulnerability and courage, she lives with nightmares in her head.

Under Hayden's patient love, Sheila slowly comes alive. Hayden fixes her hair, bathes her, teaches her hygiene. "You do be a funny lady for a teacher. I think you be as crazy as us kidses be." She follows Hayden around, wants to be cuddled. She begins to make friends, learns how to give. But she can still scream "I hate you" when frustrated, when made to do what she dislikes. Crossed, she retaliates with devastating force. In a single rampage she causes $700 damage to a classroom. When Hayden leaves for two days, Sheila goes wild; for she is afraid that, like her mother, Hayden is abandoning her, will not come back.

Antoine de Saint Exupéry's *The Little Prince* has a profound influence on Sheila, especially where the fox tells the prince: "You become responsible, forever, for what you have tamed." And Sheila looks into Hayden's eyes: "You tame me, so now you be 'sponsible for me?" And a moment later: "I tame you a little bit too, huh? And now I do be 'sponsible for you too, huh?" She shows a tremendous capacity for joy. She caresses a daffodil, the first flower anyone has ever given her: "My heart do be so big."

Just when all seems well with Sheila, her "Uncle Jerry" tries to rape her; when that fails, he cuts her deeply. "I ain't never gonna love anybody if I have to do that." And Hayden must try to get across to a six-year-old the difference between love and sexual abuse.

When Sheila is ready for a regular classroom, she doesn't want to leave. It's like another betrayal. "You're just like my Mama." Through tears Sheila sees why the dream must end. She remembers how the little prince got mad because he'd taken so much trouble to tame the fox and now the fox was crying because the little prince had to leave. "It makes you cry to tame someone, doesn't it? They kept crying in that book and I never 'xactly knew why. I always thought you only cried when someone hit you." Hayden: "You take a chance at crying when you let someone tame you." Sheila, wiping the last traces of tears away: "It still hurts a lot though, don't it?"

Some years later this came by mail:

TO TOREY WITH MUCH
"LOVE"

All the rest came
They tried to make me laugh
They played their games with me
Some games for fun and some for keeps
And then they went away
Leaving me in the ruins of games
Not knowing which were for keeps and

Which were for fun and
Leaving me alone with the echoes of
Laughter that was not mine.

Then you came
With your funny way of being
Not quite human
And you made me cry
And you didn't seem to care if I did
You just said the games are over
And waited
Until all my tears turned into
Joy.

SUMMER

The years 17 to 22 provide a transition—a bridge from adolescence to early adulthood, and a part of both. Critical years for the boy-man (or the girl-woman): I am closing out my preadult self and my place in the preadult world, and I am beginning to fashion my first adult self and to make those choices that will establish my initial membership in the adult world.

The second of human seasons (22–40) is early adulthood. It may be, as Levinson believes, the most dramatic of all the eras. From 20 to 40 is the summer of life. Heart, respiration, muscle tone, sex—a man's body is at peak strength and efficiency. Intelligence, memory, abstract thought, ability to learn specific skills, to solve well-defined problems—I am at or near the height of my powers. I make the major choices that gradually define my place in the adult world: my way of life, my style of living, my contribution to society. Early adulthood differs from the later in the fulness of its energy, in its potential for achieve-ment—but also in the external pressure that is part and parcel of it. My own inner drives and the demands of society are pow-erfully intermeshed; at times they reinforce each other, at times they stand in stark contradiction.

The summer of my content had an uncommon overture. After all, for good reasons, most humans do *not* become Jesuits. It was indeed a conversion, but not a discrete moment, al-though the conversion was symbolized on a snow-capped Feb-ruary morning when, all of eighteen years and seven months, I vowed to God perpetual poverty, chastity, and obedience. In that vowing I took the risk I did not then realize: I risked not becoming a man. By those three vows I was in danger of de-clining what the Jesuit theologian John Courtney Murray, in a famous conference to the Woodstock seminary community, called "the encounter with three elemental forces . . . encoun-ter with the earth, with woman, and with [my] own spirit." By poverty, I risked declining responsibility for my livelihood, risked "an inert, parasitic life—living off the collectivity," risked remaining irresponsible. Vowed poverty can impover-ish. By chastity, I risked refusing to enter the world of Eve, risked "adolescent senility" (sex is dead), thinking myself whole when I was not. "The pure spirit," Murray said, "can readily be the proud spirit—whose hardness makes it poor ma-terial for priestly consecration." There was the risk of remain-ing a child, the proverbial bachelor: "crotchety, emotionally unstable, petulant, and self-enclosed." By obedience, I risked declining "the most bruising encounter of all," the encounter with my own spirit and its power of choice. I risked being oth-er-directed, with my choices made for me, refusing ultimate responsibility for them. I risked "an end both to aspiration and conflict"; I could spare myself "the lonely agony of the desert struggle."

But this I did not know in 1933. In the ecstasy of kenosis,

of self-emptying in the image of God's unique Son (cf. Phil 2:7), I surrendered all that was dear to me: things, persons, my own self—everything save God. That day would in large measure determine my existence, my life style: where I lived and whom I knew, what I ate and what I wore, what I read and what I said. Oh yes, there was growth, I believe, in those early years. But, like the doctrinal development dear to old St. Vincent of Lérins, it was growth in the same line, according to a basically unvarying pattern: a deeper appreciation of vowed existence, increasing closeness to God, immersion in studies that spoke of God or led to Him, contact with people who respected my consecration.

Ordination at 26 (rather early for a Jesuit) seemed the peak of religious peaks—no crisis, no anxiety, only the feeling that now, finally, I was empowered for service, to bring God down to men and men up to God. World War II was cataclysmic, but not for me: my profession was peace, not the sword. I did not have to suffer for that conviction; FDR honored it. Nagasaki and Hiroshima left my spirit seared, but hardly third-degree burns; it was all too far away, a subject for civilized moral discourse. The body was firm, vigorous; intellectual powers were at a giddy height, centered on the Fathers of the Church. Researching and teaching, lecturing and preaching, I was making my contribution to society, defining who I was and what I could do for others.

BETWEEN SPRING AND SUMMER

For most Christians, the Jesuit experience is not their experience. The summer of their existence has different foci: a career, wife or husband, home, children. In its own fashion, however, it features crisis, experience of God, and decision. Highly significant for that summer is its prelude, its overture,

Levinson's period of transition, the bridge from adolescence to early adulthood. That is why a survey in the May 1981 issue of *Psychology Today* brought such disturbing information. From their own responses, a central passion of the 18–25 age bracket is money—at times second only to food. In consequence, many of these young people are sexually unsatisfied, in worsening health, worried and anxious, discontented with their jobs, lonely as hell.

This passion for money, understandable in an age of economic anxiety, has fascinating historical roots. Two decades ago, the distinguished sociologist Philip Rieff saw a fresh character ideal coming to dominate Western civilization. Over against the old pagan commitment to the polis, to public life, over against the Judeo-Christian commitment to a transcendent God, over against the Enlightenment commitment to the irresistible progress of reason, today's ideal type is "anti-heroic, shrewd, carefully counting his satisfactions and dissatisfactions, studying unprofitable commitments as the sins most to be avoided." The highest science? Self-concern. Devotion and self-sacrifice? Constraining ideals that must be rejected. Spiritual guidance in the best Freudian sense is "to emancipate man's 'I' from the communal 'we.'" Learn Freud's realism: conflict is embedded in human living, expectations are inevitably frustrated, life can have no all-embracing meaning, death is final.

This ideal of human living I call deadly. I'm aware of the seductive arguments—especially seductive between 18 and 25. To serve others responsibly, you had better have your own act together, get your head screwed on right. To help the underdeveloped, you must develop your own mature individuality. To give intelligently, you should have something worth giving. Before you give, you must be. Integration before self-donation.

I am moved but not convinced. A world where a billion go to bed hungry and human rights are blasted, where war rages ceaselessly and panic walks the streets, where pope and president can be shot within six weeks and atomic destruction hangs overhead—this world cannot wait for young adults to get their whole act together. If the normal product of our high schools and colleges is a man or woman simply of enlightened self-interest, these institutions are a peril to the human person.

The paradox is, the only way I can get my act together is not in isolation but in relation. I become myself to the extent that I go out of myself. I find my life in the measure that I am ready to risk it. When I can say, to a single person or to an acre of God's world, "Your life is my life," then I will begin to come alive. And beneath the touch of my love, someone else will come alive.

The transition period, then, calls for a compassionate heart. It calls, too, for an open mind. I fear much for the lawyer whose only life is corporate tax, the doctor whose whole existence is someone else's prostate, the business executive whose single responsibility is to his stockholders, the athlete who puts all his eggs in an eighteen-inch basket, the theologian who thinks the world can be saved by theology. I am afraid of men and women who claim there is only one way to God, one morality of the majority, one way to interpret the Bible or the First Amendment, even one way to say Mass—in Latin, because that's the way Jesus said it! It kills marriages and human relations, it deadens feelings and sensitivities, it makes for a society that lives in a thousand and one tunnels, with no communication and no exit.

By an open mind I do not mean a mind without fixed points, a mind that accepts everything (Marxism and capitalism, Christianity and atheism) as equally good or bad, absorbs all ideas like a sponge and is just as soft. I mean rather a realization that the life of the mind is incredibly open-ended, if only because reality is a participation in God, a reflection of Him who cannot be imprisoned in a definition.

If you are open-minded, you challenge—challenge fixed ideas, established structures, including your own. You listen—to people in other disciplines, to other ways of thinking. You don't impute evil to those with whom you disagree: they must be living in sin! You are touchingly humble, because your knowledge, however vast, is a drop in a measureless ocean. You rarely live on either–or: either creation or evolution, body or soul, church or world, liberty or law, sacred or secular, God or man, home or career, Jesus human or divine, Beethoven or Bruce Springsteen. Like the Church in its highest moments, you focus on both–and; for any decent heresy tells us something important to which we have been deaf.

Together with compassionate heart and open mind, the transition period calls for an imaginative spirit. By imagination I do not mean the fantastic, the grotesque, the bizarre. I mean the capacity we have to make the material an image of the immaterial. I mean not a "faculty" like intellect or will, but a posture of our whole person towards our experience. It is a way of seeing. It is, as with Castaneda, looking for the holes in the world or listening to the space between sounds. It is a breaking through the obvious, the surface, to the reality beneath and beyond. It is the world of intuition and wonder, of amazement and delight, of festivity and play. Concretely, it is the vision and the dream, ritual and symbol, the parable, the allegory, and the myth. It is painting and poetry, sculpture and architecture, music, dancing, and dramatic art. It is film. It is the Bible with its vast array of symbols from the creation story in Genesis through the parables of Jesus to the vision of John in the Apocalypse. It is da Vinci and e. e. cummings, Michelangelo's *Pietà* and Paolo Soleri's futuristic city in the desert, Beethoven's *Missa Solemnis* and the Beatles' *I Wanna Hold Your*

Hand. It is David whirling and skipping before the ark of the covenant, Markova dancing *Giselle.* It is Romeo forsaking his very name for Juliet. It is *Star Wars.*

I am not downgrading abstract thought, conceptual analysis, rational demonstration, scientific experiment. These are basic to liberal education. I am saying that, for your spirit to live supremely, the clear and distinct idea is not enough. Do you remember the reporters who asked Martha Graham, "What does your dance mean?" She replied: "Darlings, if I could tell you, I would not have danced it." The image is more open-ended than the concept, more susceptible of different understandings; therein lie the risk and the joy.

Often untapped between 17 and 22 is a power to reach reality we rarely mine, a capacity to grasp the true, the beautiful, and the good that has no limits. I do not predict that without imagination you will be unhappy or unsuccessful. I do claim that without it you may miss much of the thrill in human living, that you run a greater risk of finding existence unexciting, that x-number of the dead and despairing will not be quickened to life by you, that you may fail to touch in love a living God whose glory challenges not so much our logic as our imagining. For, as metaphysician Jacques Maritain insisted, the culmination of knowledge is not conceptual but experiential: man/woman "feels" God.

Compassionate heart, open mind, imaginative spirit—with such qualities you can proceed to summer with fair confidence, to fashion adult existence in the image of Christ. In the full lustiness of flesh and spirit. Aware of the Church as at once bride of Christ and adulterous. Experiencing and exploring God's works in your lives, His likeness in others, especially the crushed and the broken. Increasingly responsible for all you do and say. Between 22 and 40 you create the Christian man and woman. In these two decades you can discover, in unique fashion, the God who gave joy to your youth. Whatever the web of relationships, whatever the level of your material existence, here is the creative segment of your human existence, your religious existence. Now is when you are most likely to find yourself, to discover the I.

My several years as theologian-in-residence at Georgetown University have updated my understanding of these transitional years. On the one hand, my experience confirms the results of recent research into collegians' attitudes and values—conclusions that should be of interest and concern to churches and church-related schools. More and more students are coming to college with their values already fixed; the colleges are having less and less impact on student values. The church is seen by college youth rather as a resource than as an authority in their lives. Catholic collegians pay little regard to the moral teaching of the magisterium, especially in sexual areas. Many declare themselves Catholic while rejecting any obligation to "go to church" unless they feel like going.

On the other hand, I am ceaselessly moved, thrilled, humbled by the profound spirituality and social concern of many Georgetown students—and this in the midst of a pleasure-loving culture and a drug-addicted, so-called "mercenary" generation. Many have an intense prayer life, know and love Jesus as a real person, joy in genuine liturgy. A good number move out to the poor and downtrodden, the helpless and hopeless, from 14th Street in Washington through Appalachia to Central America. Just before graduation two years ago, a gifted, attractive, high-spirited senior told a worshiping community on this campus: "Georgetown has opened my eyes to the rest of the world. I feel an obligation to give something of what I've been given." Several months later Mary Beth was off to India, on funds she had begged, to share her nursing competence and her compassion with the poor and the sick.

At times our young-in-transition reveal a courage beyond human comprehension. I read recently a brief obituary of

Terry Fox, dead of cancer at 22. In 1977 his right leg was amputated and he became a thin boy in a wheel chair. His former basketball coach showed him an article about a one-legged man in the New York Marathon, and Terry began to build his body and perfect the stride that came to be called the "Fox Trot." On April 12, 1980, Terry began his Canadian "marathon of hope," a coast-to-coast run on an artificial leg to publicize the fight against cancer and raise money for research. Four and a half months and 3,317 miles later, with $24 million raised, he had to stop. The cancer had spread to his lungs, he was hospitalized, pneumonia set in, and Terry Fox died—a deathless symbol, to Canada and the world, of courage and of hope. "I wanted to show people that just because they're disabled, it's not the end."

CRISIS, EXPERIENCE, DECISION

The summer of Christian life features crisis, experience of God, and decision. There is no single path the journey takes; not even a Jesuit can program your pilgrimage in advance. The legendary Antony sells all he has and spends the next 85 years searching for solitude; Thomas More, after four years with the Carthusians, decides to wear his hair shirt in the world and seek his God through the world. At 22, Luther is flung violently to the ground by a lightning bolt and vows to St. Anne that he will enter a monastery; 12 years later he nails his 95 theses to the castle church in Wittenberg; three years after that, he burns the bull of his excommunication. The examples of Christian summer are as varied as the men and women who live that season. It may help to sketch several of the more striking, yet not unique, experiences with a bit of detail.

I am, quite naturally, attracted to St. Ignatius Loyola, contemporary of Luther and founder of the Society of Jesus. Almost 30, he was still uncertain what God wanted of him. Gone was the Basque caballero, enamored of courtly love, full of high spirits and laughter, the free lance who had put his sword at the service of Charles I and the Duke of Nájera. He had been vanquished with the battle of Pamplona, when a shattered leg forced a convalescence that brought him face to face, no longer with romantic chivalry, but with the exploits of a Dominic and a Francis of Assisi. What they had done he too would do.

The course of Ignatius' life, the course of Christian existence for countless men and women still to be born, was largely determined a year later (1522). In the walled and towered town of Manresa, Ignatius lived eleven months as a hermit. Daily, it seems, he retired to his holy cave (really a huge overhanging shelf of rock open in the front) to pray in solitude and do penance in secret. Three stages marked this experience. The first four months were a purifying fire: penances, vigils, a slovenly exterior—above all, a surrender to prayer—all this in a state of high happiness. The second stage involved dark nights of the soul; what had formerly delighted him gave him joy no longer. Scruples afflicted him; his past sins tormented him; he was even tempted to suicide. But it was also the beginning of soul-stirring changes he had never experienced before. He was starting to distinguish between good and bad spirits; consolation and desolation followed hard on one another.

The third stage was the most important. One day in August or September, Ignatius walked out of Manresa to visit an outlying church. The road followed the edge of a steep hillside, at the foot of which flows the Cardoner River. On the way, he sat down for a while facing the river below. As he sat there, his mind began to open like a flower. It was not a vision; Ignatius insists on that. Rather, he understood spiritual and temporal realities with such astounding clarity that everything seemed new to him. He was never able to spell out the contents of that

illumination in detail. He did indeed confide later to dear colleagues that it had largely to do with God One and Three, with
the fashioning of the world and the bodying forth of the Son.
But even after three decades it was not so much the what as
the how that astonished him, the fresh clarity in his understanding—such clarity that this one experience outstripped all
else he learned or was given by God in sixty-two years. Small
wonder that after a while the pilgrim Ignatius rose to his feet,
walked over to a wayside cross, and knelt to give thanks to his
new-found God.

Manresa was for Ignatius what Damascus was for Paul, the
burning bush for Moses: a mystery-laden self-manifestation of
God that initiated and synthesized his mission, a call to set
forth on a shadowed road that would keep opening up as he
kept following it. The experience transformed him. Not only
on the outside: more presentable and sociable, less harsh and
rigid, more human. On a deeper level, it was his inner life that
altered. A spirituality that had been individualistic and intro-
spective turned increasingly communitarian and apostolic.
The Ignatius who had planned a pilgrimage to Jerusalem main-
ly to do penance was now yearning rather to meet Christ in
the places where he had lived and died, to walk literally in his
footsteps.

Ignatius' experience exemplifies a fascinating phenome-
non. I have remarked it in others, remember it vividly from
my own early years as a Jesuit. The first steps in conscious
Christian conversion often stress purgation and purification—
the "purgative way" of classical spiritual writers. In my novice-
ship, and for several years after, asceticism and self-denial had
a high priority. By mortification and meditation we tried to
root out the effects of sin and sinfulness in our lives. It touched
every facet of our existence. We rose and retired, prayed and
played, at the sound of a bell. We ate like healthy young animals, but passed up the sweets and left something "for the an-

gels." We guarded our eyes scrupulously not only from the sensual and the lewd but also from much that was legitimate. We lashed our backs with knotted cords at bedtime (it rarely did more than tingle), wore a chain on the thigh till after breakfast (one novice seemed uncommonly impervious to pain, till we discovered he wore it over his heavy underwear). Excessive laughter was a no-no, a sad face discouraged, a furrowed brow frowned on.

However bizarre it may seem in the 80's, the asceticism had merit; usually it was our immaturity that made for scars. In point of fact, it corresponded rather nicely to the First Week of Ignatius' own Spiritual Exercises, a solid preparation for the Second Week, where the stress is on Christ: to know him more clearly, love him more dearly, follow him more nearly.

There is no predicting the path along which an experience of God will lead you. Take Simone Weil again. Daughter of free-thinking Jews, she grew up in complete agnosticism. Never did she enter a synagogue, never witness a Jewish ceremony. Hers from earliest years was the Christian, French, Greek tradition.

Almost 29, she spent ten days at the Benedictine Abbey of Solesmes, from Palm Sunday to Easter Tuesday, following the liturgical services. There she met a young English Catholic, who introduced her to the metaphysical poets of the seventeenth century. Reading them later on, she discovered what is surely the famous poem of George Herbert known as "Love (III)":

> Love bade me welcome: yet my soul drew back,
>   Guiltie of dust and sinne.
> But quick-ey'd Love, observing me grow slack
>   From my first entrance in,
> Drew nearer to me, sweetly questioning,
>   If I lack'd any thing.

A guest, I answer'd, worthy to be here:
    Love said, You shall be he.
I the unkinde, ungratefull? Ah my deare,
    I cannot look on thee.
Love took my hand, and smiling did reply,
    Who made the eyes but I?

Truth Lord, but I have marr'd them: let my shame
    Go where it doth deserve.
And know you not, sayes Love, who bore the blame?
    My deare, then I will serve.
You must sit down, sayes Love, and taste my meat:
    So I did sit and eat.

This poem Simone learned by heart. Often, when a violent headache reached its peak, she would say it over and over again, concentrating all her attention on it, clinging to its tenderness with all her soul. In the beginning she thought only that she was reciting a beautiful poem, but without her knowing it the poem had the virtue of a prayer. During one of those recitations "Christ himself came down and took possession of me."

Before that experience, Simone had heard but never believed that a person-to-person contact between a human being and God was possible on earth. Accounts of apparitions, like the miracles recorded in the Gospels, had turned her off. But "in this sudden possession of me by Christ, neither my senses nor my imagination had any part; I only felt in the midst of my suffering the presence of a love, like that which one can read in the smile on a beloved face."

A transforming experience indeed, but hardly her last. Late in life (she only lived to be 34) she was entranced by the "infinite sweetness" of the Our Father in Greek. She used to recite it each day before work in the vineyard, repeat it often through the day, made it a practice to say it once each morning "with absolute attention." The effect was extraordinary. At times the first words tore her thoughts from her body, transported it outside space. Filling every part of an "infinity of infinity," there was silence, a silence that was not an absence of sound but object of a positive sensation. "Sometimes, also during this recitation or at other moments, Christ is present with me in person, but his presence is infinitely more real, more moving, more clear than on that first occasion when he took possession of me."

Transforming experiences—of God, of Christ, of Catholicism, of the Mass. And still Simone never seriously considered being baptized or becoming a Christian, a Catholic. Why not? Because, as she saw it, the Church, as catholic, should contain all vocations without exception. But it did not. So many things that she loved and did not want to give up, "so many things that God loves," were outside the Church. And so, since Christianity was catholic by right but not in fact, she saw it as legitimate for her to be a member of the Church by right but not in fact—for her whole life if need be. Not merely legitimate but her duty, as long as God did not clearly order her to do anything else. She would betray the truth as she saw it, if she left the point where she had been since her birth, "at the intersection of Christianity and everything that is not Christianity."

An insurmountable obstacle to such an incarnation of Christianity Simone found in two little words: *anathema sit.* Not their existence but their employment. This prevented her from crossing the threshold of the Church. She had to remain beside all those things that cannot enter the Church on account of those two little words. She had to remain beside them all the more because her own intelligence was numbered among them.

Simone was convinced that the Spirit of truth speaks two distinct languages, depending on circumstances, and the two languages simply do not agree: the collective language and the

individual one, the language Christ used before an assembly
and the language he used to a beloved friend. "When genuine
friends of God ... repeat words they have heard in secret
amidst the silence of the union of love, and these words are in
disagreement with the teaching of the Church, it is simply that
the language of the market place is not that of the nuptial
chamber." Simone was convinced that, with God's help, she
could bear witness that without the joy of membership in the
Mystical Body of Christ, one can still be faithful to him unto
death. For that reason, among others, she has been styled "the
saint of the churchless."

To my embarrassment now, I cannot recall an "experience of God" in my young adulthood. I am reluctant to conclude I did not have one; for I suspect that my basic fidelity to
priestly existence in the Society of Jesus could hardly have
been sustained without it. Perhaps it is a matter of words. We
were not encouraged to seek an "experience" of God. We did
indeed know of such experiences. How could we not? There
was Moses before the burning bush, and God addressing Jere-
miah. There was Jesus on the Mount of Transfiguration, and
Paul thrown by God from his horse. There was the experience
of Augustine and Monica at Ostia: "we did for one instant at-
tain to touch" Wisdom. There were the mystics: Julian of Norwich and Teresa of Avila, Mechtild of Magdeburg and
Catherine of Siena, Ruysbroeck and Ramón Lull, Bridget of
Sweden and Hildegarde of Bingen. There was Ignatius at the
Cardoner. And there was scholasticism in the Thomist style,
starting not with God but with experience.

Still, we were not urged to yearn for such experiences.
Two forces, I suggest, were at play here. On the one hand,
there was the thesis (not unchallenged in the theological and
spiritual literature) that this sort of contact with God was not
what the ordinary Christian was called to; not to this did humble souls aspire. Ours was rather the more tranquil movement

of trusting faith, quickened by meditation and sacraments. On the other hand, the very word "experience" had a suspect ancestry: it conjured up Montanism and Modernism, Kant and Schleiermacher, unbridled subjectivism. It had a "Protestant" ring to it.

Oh yes, we were urged to be aware of our new life in Christ, of Father, Son, and Spirit dynamically present within us. But the stress lay on the ontological reality of grace, not on the personal and quasi-intuitive awareness of what takes place psychologically in our consciousness. Not for us the concerns of Marcel and Lavelle; it was not yet the age of Rahner and Schillebeeckx.

Crisis, experience of God, decision—these facets of early adulthood are strikingly transparent in Augustine. No single thinker has influenced Western culture so profoundly and on so many fronts. And yet, till he was 32, Augustine was just another bright young man in tortured quest of truth and love. Born to a Christian mother and a pagan father, unbaptized, with only a superficial knowledge of Christ and Christianity, he had to confront two major crises quite unprepared. One crisis was moral, the other intellectual.

The moral crisis had begun early, when Augustine was 15: "Arrived now at adolescence, I burned for all the satisfactions of hell, and I sank to the animal in a succession of dark lusts." At 16 he came to semipagan Carthage; there "a cauldron of illicit loves leapt and boiled about me. I was not yet in love, but I was in love with love." At 17 he took a mistress, lived with her for 13 years, had a son by her, surrendered her with sorrow: "My heart . . . was broken and wounded and shed blood." During this prolonged crisis Augustine's prayer to God was touchingly expressive of his inner conflict: " 'Grant me chastity and continence, but not yet.' For I was afraid that you would hear my prayer too soon, and too soon would heal me."

The intellectual crisis began when Augustine was 18, in

transition to young adulthood. He had read Cicero, and from
that moment he thirsted for truth and wisdom. This truth and
wisdom he sought in Scripture, but the Bible repelled him: it
was too simple, could not compare with the majesty of Cicero.
Catholicism seemed naive—good enough for his mother Monica, unworthy of an intellectual. What beguiled him was Manicheism, the religion of the Persian prophet Mani.

Manichean propaganda proved a powerful magnet. It
lured Augustine's intellectualism, for it claimed to be scientific,
a revelation demonstrated by reason, a free philosophy without the bridle of faith. It tempted the sophisticate: here was
salvation through secret knowledge. It preserved the relics of
his childhood religion: here was a superior, perfect form of
Christianity, completing the revelation of Christ. It touched an
inner torment: perhaps the origin of evil could be explained by
two Principles at war, the Good and the Evil. It appealed to his
pride, for it absolved him from moral guilt: a strange Principle,
another nature, was responsible for his sin. "It pleased my
pride to be free from blame."

It took ten years of Manicheism to disenchant Augustine.
Even then orthodox Christianity did not seem the answer.
Skepticism tempted him lightly. And he still had to learn that a
captivating philosophy, Neoplatonism, did not possess the two
truths he needed, the twin truths he found in St. Paul: a God
who saves man by becoming man, and a grace which alone
gives victory over sin. And even when he had discovered the
Savior Christ and his grace, it was Augustine's intellect that
was captured; his will was not completely conquered—the pull
of the flesh was still too powerful.

The drama reached its climax in August of 386. The city
was Milan, the scene a little garden. "There I was, going mad
on my way to sanity, dying on my way to life, aware how evil I
was, unaware that I was to grow better in a little while." Pleasure plucked at his garment of flesh, murmuring softly: "Are

you sending us away?" Chastity smiled on him and gave him courage: "Cast yourself upon the Lord and be not afraid." Conscious of his sinfulness, he was torn by violent tears and flung himself down beneath a fig tree: "How long shall I go on saying 'tomorrow'?" Suddenly he heard a voice from a nearby house; "it was sort of sing-song, repeated again and again, 'Take and read, take and read.'" Interpreting the incident as a divine command to open his book of Scripture, he snatched it up and read in silence the passage on which his eyes first fell: "not in revelry and drunkenness, not in debauchery and wantonness, not in strife and jealousy; but put on the Lord Jesus Christ, and as for the flesh, take no thought for its lusts" (Rom 13:13–14). At that moment "it was as though a light of utter confidence shone in all my heart, and all the darkness of uncertainty vanished away."

Almost nine months later, on the night between Holy Saturday and Easter Sunday 387, Augustine was baptized by the Bishop of Milan, St. Ambrose. That night the oil of confirmation completed his baptism, and for the first time Augustine pillowed on his tongue the Christ he had fled for 17 years. It was a historic night for the Western world.

STRUGGLE AND REAPPRAISAL

Frequently, crisis and decision are not "one shot" affairs, with the decisive moment ending the struggle once for all. At times, decisions demand reappraisal: witness the agonizing reassessments of lifetime commitments to marriage or ministry. Even where the decision is not revoked, it is often the prelude to a long, hot summer. A moving example is the American composer Gian Carlo Menotti. His opera *The Saint of Bleecker Street* (1954) deals with the conflict among saintly Annina (mysticism), her unbelieving brother Michele (cynical realism), and his mistress Desideria (earthly love). In their efforts to convert one another, they succeed only in destroying one another. The opera is a reflection of Menotti himself, of his struggle with faith and the Catholic Church. He has described his own situation poignantly:

> I am definitely *not* a religious man. All the same I am haunted by religious problems, as most of my works show. Why? I can hardly explain it to myself. Can one be a secular mystic? Since the age of 16 I had broken away from the Catholic Church, and I very much doubt, as some of my wishful religious friends predict, that at the last minute I shall ask for Extreme Unction and the holy sacraments.
>
> However, it is undeniable that the intense and incandescent faith which nourished my childhood and my adolescence has seared my soul forever. I've lost my faith, but it is a loss that has left me uneasy. I often feel like a runaway, who suddenly finds himself wondering if he has not left home too rashly or too soon. A certain nostalgia for my years of grace is, I believe, the knowledge that faith cannot be attained, but can only be given by God as an act of grace. But alas, or fortunately, depending on how you look at it, my mind is much too rational to abandon itself to faith. I am a would-be Voltaire, yearning to be Tolstoy, if you know what I mean. And it is this very duality in my character, this inner conflict, which I have tried to express in some of my operas. First in "The Medium" and then, and foremost, in "The Saint of Bleecker Street."

Menotti claims that *The Saint* pinpointed the psychological and religious ambiguities that had always been part of him.

> I have been accused of leaving the theme of "The Saint of Bleecker Street" unresolved. On whose side am I? Michele the unbeliever, or Annina the saint? But of course, I cannot take sides, because I am both. I am Michele, who envies Annina. That is why I have depicted their love as almost incestuous. The opera symbolizes my own inner conflict—the split in my personality—the impossibility of being both.

The disillusionment that began for Menotti in adolescence can strike the young adult even more rudely. Earlier ideals, beliefs, hopes, allegiances come into conflict with soul-shattering realities. It may be a war that fragments a body or a mind, an atomic bomb that fashions a new hell in Hiroshima. It may be a marriage that has turned sour, a crib child who has stopped breathing. It may be a church that has gone too far too fast, or too slow and not far enough. It may be a job terminated, love betrayed. The causes are legion, and the outcome for different people is hardly predictable.

In Elie Wiesel's sensitive story *The Gates of the Forest,* the protagonist Gregor, who has experienced so much of Jewish suffering, meets a powerful Rebbe. "And Auschwitz?" Gregor asks. "What do you make of Auschwitz?" "Auschwitz," the Rebbe replies, "proves that nothing has changed, that the primeval war goes on. Man is capable of love and hate, murder and sacrifice. He is Abraham and Isaac together." Gregor grows angry: "After what happened to us, how can you believe in God?" And the Rebbe answers with an understanding smile: "How can you *not* believe in God after what has happened?"

This is not simply a striking story; nor is it just a Jewish problem. It illustrates the other side of the human coin: the experience of evil. If experience of God lifts us above ourselves, experience of evil can shatter us. For better or worse, my experience of evil has been largely at evil's edge. I have heard about it, read of it, seen it on TV. As for so long I knew *about* God, so most of my early life I knew *about* evil. I did not come face to face with it, as did Anne Frank or Daniel Berrigan. If I struggled with evil, it was not in the public arena, hand to hand, eyeball to eyeball. I confronted war and sin, destitution and discrimination, injustice and oppression largely in the relatively safe tower of the mind. Most closely, behind a microphone or before a typewriter.

WHO AM I?

Quite often our young-adult crises are not so much conflicts with evil as struggles to determine our identity: Who am I
and how do I become me? That critical effort transpires strikingly in one of the major poets of the Victorian era, the Jesuit
Gerard Manley Hopkins (1844–89). A discerning critic, John
Pick, has declared that in Hopkins' life "there is really only one
date of great significance: the year 1868 when he entered the
Jesuit Order. This marks the turning-point of his life and di-
vides his youth from his maturity, his adolescence from his
manhood. It also marks the division between his early verse
and his great poetry."

Some have mistakenly seen Hopkins' summer (the only
adult season of his existence) as a ceaseless, agonizing, unre-
solved conflict between poet and priest: either he was a splen-
did poet despite his Jesuit discipline and spirituality, or his
conversion and vocation throttled a promising artistry.

Superficially, indeed, some evidence can be interpreted in
this vein. Some months before his definitive decision to become a priest, he wrote his friend A. W. M. Baillie that such a
decision would mean virtually the death of his poetry: "I want
to write still and as a priest I very likely can do that too, not so
freely as I shd. have liked, e.g. nothing or little in the verse
way, but no doubt what wd. best serve the cause of my religion." His decision at 24 to join the Jesuits coincided with a
poignant, cryptic entry in his Journal: "Slaughter of the innocents." The "innocents" were his poems, the children he had
fathered; those "innocents" he burned. A decade later he
would write to Canon R. W. Dixon: "What I had written I
burnt before I became a Jesuit and resolved to write no more,
as not belonging to my profession, unless it were by the wish of
my superiors." For seven years after he entered the Jesuit Or-

der Hopkins wrote no poetry. After writing "The Wreck of the Deutschland" in 1875 at the suggestion of his rector, "I held myself free to compose, but cannot find it in my conscience to spend time upon it; so I have done little and shall do less. . . . But even the impulse to write is wanting, for I have no thought of publishing."

The quotations are reminiscent of St. Jerome's famous dream almost 1500 years before. This passionate humanist dreamt himself haled before Christ on a serious charge: "You are not a Christian, you are a Ciceronian." In consequence, he swore never again to read books of pagan literature. How faithful Jerome remained to his vow, made in a moment of strong emotional stress, is not clear. Happily, he did not need to reread his favorite classics to be influenced by them. He was so steeped in classical culture that he confessed he could no more forget it than the wine jar can lose the flavor of the wine.

The problem is, isolated quotations from Hopkins can be deceptive. The poet-priest issue can only be understood where it was actually resolved: in the context of Hopkins' central concern. I mean his struggle for perfection in line with a fundamental principle in the Spiritual Exercises of St. Ignatius: whatever I elect to do, I elect it because it helps me to the end for which I have been created—to praise, reverence, and serve God. Poetry could not be an end in itself; it had to be a servant.

Hopkins' deeper struggle, therefore, was for Christian maturity—growing into the image of the Christ who did not do his own will but the will of his Father, even unto crucifixion. His poetry was symbolic of that growth and accompanied it. Oh yes, he wrote less than if he had been primarily a poet; but what he did write is impressively expressive of an extraordinarily sensitive man, arguably more intense than it would have been outside the religious context.

There was movement, questioning, soul-searching; there

was change; there were peaks and valleys. From the twenty-two-year-old's sense-denying asceticism, "Be shellèd, eyes, with double dark/ And find the uncreated light," he moved in four years to a sacramental view of nature, finding the beauty of the Lord in the bluebell and the starlight—here akin to Duns Scotus and Ignatius Loyola. The great ode "The Wreck of the Deutschland," born not from the prompting of superiors but from the rich seven-year silence, is, in a sense, his own story, his spiritual struggles, as he felt God's finger and the call to the cross of "*Ipse,* the only one, Christ." Ten of his most delightful, joy-packed poems were written in the months just before and after his ordination—lyrical affirmations of the world as "word, expression, news, of God." Parish work in London and Liverpool, in Bedford Leigh and Glasgow, left him little time for writing, left him depressed over the ugliness and hollowness of nineteenth-century civilization, over industrialism's blight on natural beauty and the human soul: "all is seared with trade; bleared, smeared with toil;/ And wears man's smudge and shares man's smell." As he moved among his people, a new tenderness, a fresh concern, invaded his poems: "Life all laced in the other's,/ Lóve-laced!"

Hopkins' final five years, teaching classics and examining in Dublin, were marked with poor health and nervous fatigue, with an anxiety and a melancholy that at its worst he compared to madness. It was a situation that made poetry exceptionally difficult. And still the poems of 1884–89 are profoundly expressive of his religious life. Mortal beauty is admirable indeed, but it must be crowned by "God's better beauty, grace." Seven sonnets of desolation are dredged from his "winter world," wrung from a burdened body and wearied mind, from his aridity, the feeling that God has withdrawn His love.

Only if you can see Hopkins laying his life and his poetry

gladly at the foot of the cross, can you read without surprise his deathbed words at 45: "I am so happy, I am so happy, I am so happy."

Hopkins' effort (in the main successful, I would think) to harmonize priest and poet, or to subsume poetry under priesthood, raises a broader question. It is an issue that, like a gadfly, returns time and again to torment the front-line priest and the speculative theologian. How justify so many of a priest's activities since the great Catholic immigrations, from the bricks and mortar of his church to the parish softball team? The problem became more prickly for us when the so-called hyphenated priest (priest-educator, priest-scientist, priest-worker) was called into question. Is it not the laity's task to baptize "the world," to sacralize the secular? Was I not ordained to offer sacrifice and to forgive sin?

In the 60's and early 70's the issue ceased to be academic; you might say it turned ugly. The priestly emphasis had been on functions, on roles. We defined an ordained priest in terms of what he could *do* which an unordained person could not do. Here the crisis of identity tore the guts of uncounted priests, especially in their late summer or early autumn. Many searched for the meaning of their ministry in terms of something specific to themselves, powers proper to priests, functions that distinguished them from laymen. But what they alone could do ("This is my body," "I absolve you") took so little of their time, so little of their life. The rest of their existence— preaching, teaching, building, organizing, counseling, and what not—was lived in the suspicion that some man or woman in the pews could do it better.

This acute crisis in identity forced many of us to reconsider our theology of priesthood. What does it mean to be an ordained priest? This is not the place to spell out the possible responses. I, for one, was persuaded that we must go behind Church function to Church office. Not office in the sense of bureaucratic structure. Church office here is a relationship of responsibility. The essence of my priesthood is a new relation to the mission of the Church. The community, declaring that it sees in me the basic competences and spiritual gifts desirable for the Church's mission at this moment in history, trusts me to be its representative leader in its official actions. For my part, I have engaged myself publicly to a life of dedicated service in an official capacity, have professed my willingness to shape my life to the needs of the gospel as the Church sees them. I am now a *public* servant, in a sense in which the layperson can rarely be.

What is it that priestly office demands of me, what public service? One service, one responsibility, before all else. Since the Church's mission is to reconcile all men and women with God and with one another through the one mediator Christ, my primary office is to be a personal, living, effective sign, witness, agent of the reconciling Christ who works through me.

Because this is not simply my Christian calling but my public office, I can be called to account for the clarity, authenticity, and wholeness of my witness. The community can demand of me a certain level of performance, a ceaseless reaching for heights of holiness, a way of life that reflects the Christ who was so utterly human, yet more than human. Because much has been given to me, by Christ and the community, much can be expected of me.

Basic to my growing understanding of ordained ministry is this conviction: it is impossible to draw up two lists, one of specifically priestly works, the other of nonpriestly activities. The work I do is a priestly work if it is a work to which the Church calls me at this concrete juncture. Apart from sin, there is no radically profane area in human existence—not after God took our flesh and touched our world with His fingers and His footsteps. In sanctuary or Congress, in chemistry lab or on picket line, I am playing priest as long as I am carrying out, witnessing to, what the Church asks of me at this moment in her mission. Whether it is the Church that is calling is not always easy to discern, but the principle itself is clear, and the principle is highly significant for priesthood today.

Consequently, I have no difficulty recognizing priestly activity in the decade that Robert Drinan spent in the House of Representatives (I recall a columnist's remark when Rome ordered him not to run for re-election in 1980: "Father Drinan is doing wholesale what Mother Teresa is doing retail"). I see the priest in George Higgins' four decades with labor-management issues, even though some fine Catholics do not agree with all he said and did; in Daniel Berrigan's struggle for peace, his witness behind bars and in verse, however one may react to individual acts; in Andrew Greeley's sociological studies, despite the furor over *Cardinal Sins.* I see no contradiction in a white-jacketed Jesuit running genetics tests at Georgetown University Hospital, or in a Roman collar wilting in the classroom under the passionate poetry of Sappho.

Their decisions were responses to concrete needs, in the context of the Church's mission. On broad lines and in their essence, these decisions have the Church's blessing and these men represent her, even though not every action of theirs is necessarily representative of her—any more than my official commission to preach the Word commits the Church to every word I preach. Such decisions are often difficult to make, especially if the priest is sensitive to their awesome consequences, for himself and for the community he supposedly represents; they can and do divide the Church. It only confirms what needs no confirmation: neither priesthood nor Christianity is for the fainthearted or the simpleton.

An analogous problem in identity confronts the dedicated young layman and laywoman. What role ought the laity to play in the Church and in the world? Here, paradoxically, a major obstacle has been the Roman Catholic Church itself. We have

come a long way from the infamous letter of Msgr. George Tal-
bot, adviser to Pius X on English affairs, to Archbishop Man-
ning of Westminster: "What is the province of the laity? To
hunt, to shoot, to entertain. These matters they understand,
but to meddle in ecclesiastical affairs they have no right at all."
We have come a long way from the strong affirmation of Pius
X himself: "In the hierarchy alone reside the power and the
authority necessary to move and direct all the members of the
society to its end. As for the many, they have no other right
than to let themselves be guided and so follow their pastors in
docility." No ... other ... right. We have come a long way
from our semifacetious definition of Catholic Action in mid-
century: "the participation of the laity in the inactivity of the
hierarchy."

Many movements helped. In the 1930's the Young Christian Workers dynamized Europe by consciously bearing gospel
witness in the whole area of work. World War II, captivity, the
fraternity of distress, the comradeship of the Resistance led laity to a profound awareness that they have an active role in the
Church that demands initiative, boldness, even at times resistance and rebellion. Theologians like Yves Congar were pa-
tiently, learnedly constructing a theology of the laity that
stresses the basic equality of all the baptized in Christ and the
Spirit, the single community of faith and love with an astounding diversity of charisms, the intimate share of the laity in the
priestly, prophetic, and royal mission of Christ and his Church.
These efforts have borne rich fruit in Vatican II's Decree on
the Apostolate of the Laity and in chapter 4 of its Dogmatic
Constitution on the Church. The Council even includes this
rare acknowledgment, inserted during the final drafting of the
document on the laity: "Since in our times women have an
ever more active share in the whole life of society, it is very
important that they participate more widely also in the various
fields of the Church's apostolate" (no. 9).

All well and good—in principle. But in the arena of blood-and-guts reality, young Catholic adults are often puzzled, even dismayed, at the Church's seeming refusal to take them seriously at the very core of their apostolic life and activity. Even apart from the highly inflammatory issue of ordination, women are still largely second-class citizens, with little impact on decisions that affect their human and religious existence. The experiences of faith-full husbands and wives, however profound and poignant and perduring, apparently carry no theological significance if they clash with established teaching. Doctors and health-care administrators are told in ecclesiastical directives: "The moral evaluation of new scientific developments and *legitimately debated questions* must be finally submitted to the teaching authority of the Church in the person of the local bishop." On the other hand, I take heart from recent efforts to involve lay experts in the tortuous effort to assay the morality of nuclear weaponry. More generally, I am encouraged by a fresh turn in episcopal statements: less often a definitive decree, increasingly a challenge to the Christian conscience.

These latter remarks are not impertinent to the summer of Christian existence; quite the contrary. If, as I have suggested, this segment of life is characterized by crisis, experience of God, and decision, the search for responsible roles within the Church may be crucial for a large number of the intelligent laity. Here Vatican II's Pastoral Constitution on the Church in the Modern World is right on target: "Let the layperson not imagine that his/her pastors are always such experts that to every problem which arises, however complicated, they can readily give him/her a concrete solution, or even that such is their mission. Rather, enlightened by Christian wisdom and giving close attention to the teaching authority of the Church, let the layman/laywoman take on his/her own distinctive role" (no. 43).

Not a simple task for the young adult: to grow into the responsible freedom of the children of God.

WHEN SUMMER IS FINALE

As with Simone Weil, so for all too many, the summer of life can be dreadfully short, with no autumn, no winter. My only brother died at 27 of intestinal cancer, three weeks after the death of our father, himself only 53. Even then it all seemed so unreal, because I was closeted in a seminary during most of his dying. We had shared grade school and high school, but for the next decade I did not really know him; Jesuit scholastics were then rigidly separated from home and family. And so I do not know what Eddie's thoughts were, his ambitions, his crises and his decisions, his loves and his hates, what hurt him and what made him laugh. I have only dim recollections of courage beyond the ordinary.

It is strange that I know much more about someone I never knew, a man who died in London in 1890 at the age of 26. He has come to life as "The Elephant Man" of stage and screen. When a compassionate surgeon, Frederick Treves, first saw him, John Merrick was 20. He was terribly misshapen, "the most disgusting specimen of humanity" Treves had ever seen. Giant nodes extended his head like masses of dough; its circumference was no less than his waist. Another mass of bone protruded like a pink stump from his mouth, making of it only a slobbering aperture, turning speech into torture. From his back hung sack-like masses of flesh covered by a kind of loathsome cauliflower skin; from his chest, a bag of flesh "like a dewlap suspended from the neck of a lizard." A hip disease had left him permanently lame, unable to walk without a stick.

When Treves came upon him, by accident or providence,

Merrick was a circus freak, exploited for his ability to shock, to make people throw up; he had no other way to live. "He was shunned like a leper," Treves recalled, "housed like a wild beast, and got his only view of the world from a peephole in a showman's cart."

Two years later, Treves housed Merrick in the London Hospital, with his own bed-sitting room and a bathroom. Merrick, he discovered, was highly intelligent, acutely sensitive, romantically imaginative. Against all the odds, his genetic disorder and the cruelty of his fellows had not embittered him. He was gentle and affectionate, free of cynicism and resentment, with never an unkind word for anyone.

Merrick was even able to face others without embarrassment. That transformation began when a young widow entered his room, wished him good morning, and shook his hand. Merrick sobbed uncontrollably: apart from his mother, she was the first woman who had ever smiled at him, ever touched his hand. From then on he lost his shyness, loved to see his door open and the world flock to him—ladies of note in the social world, actress Madge Kendal, Queen Alexandra (then Princess of Wales). Alexandra's signed photograph he wept over, framed, revered like an ikon. And one evening he satisfied a burning thirst: he saw his first play, shadowed in a private box of Drury Lane Theatre, screened by nurses in front dressed in evening gowns. The pantomime left him enraptured; for here, as Treves noted, "was a being with the brain of a man, the fancies of a youth and the imagination of a child." After three years and four months in London Hospital, death came unexpectedly for Merrick—possibly from a dislocated neck, in trying to sleep "like other people."

Time and again before that tragic April afternoon, "the elephant man" had told Treves: "I am happy every hour of the day." How is it that such physical deformation, such pain and humiliation, did not lead to a deformed personality? It did for the poet Alexander Pope, a terribly misshapen dwarf, corrosively preoccupied with his deformities, despite advantages Merrick never had. For one thing, Ashley Montagu thinks it highly likely that Merrick received much love from his mother during the significant early years of his life (she died when he was 12); without such love his personality would be difficult to explain. But we must allow for the possibility that he did not experience such love; the evidence is not compelling. If so, we might have to conclude, with Montagu, that in common with those whose childhood was demonstrably loveless and who still emerged relatively undamaged, his genetic constitution "was exceptionally resistant to the privations of mothering that most children require for adequately healthy behavioral development."

John Merrick confounds so many of our pet theories about personality, about human living, about good and evil. He exemplifies, quite rudely, how much potentiality for life and love, for joy and laughter, lies deep within the scarred and disfigured, needing only a smile or a touch to release it. I suspect that a Jew or a Christian might further be reminded of Solomon's Wisdom 4:8–16:

> The age that is honorable comes not
>   with the passing of time,
> Nor can it be measured
>   in terms of years.
> Rather, count a man grey-haired
>   when he is wise,
> Ripe of age,
>   when his life is stainless.
> Divine favor, divine love banished him
>   from a life he shared with sinners;
> Caught him away,
>   before wickedness could pervert his
>   thoughts,
>   before wrong-doing could allure his heart.

Such witchery evil has,
    to tarnish honor,
Such alchemy do the roving passions exercise
    even on minds that are true metal.
With him, early achievement
    counted for long apprenticeship;
So well the Lord loved him,
    from a corrupt world He would grant him
      swift release.
The world looks on,
    uncomprehending;
A hard lesson it is to learn,
    that God does reward,
    does pity His chosen friends,
    does grant His faithful servants deliverance.
Did they know it,
    the death of the just man,
    with its promise early achieved,
Is a reproach to the wicked that live yet,
    unregarded in their late old age.

What is regrettably absent from Merrick's story is any evidence of religious influence on his personality. Oh yes, God's grace and love were there—in abundance. Otherwise how could this sensitive man have come to terms with such flawed humanity? But nowhere does he speak of Him who shaped him so strangely in His own image—save perhaps in the magnificent model of a church he constructed with one hand from colored paper and cardboard. The Bible and Prayer Book, Treves tells us, he knew "intimately." But whether the Psalms he knew so well taught him to trust a God ever faithful to the disadvantaged and despised; whether he related in love to the Jesus who "had no form or comeliness that we should look at him, and no beauty that we should desire him" (Isa 53:2); whether belief in resurrection offset the unsightliness of his earthly flesh—on this, history is mute.

That is why, despite my admiration for this good and gentle Christ-figure, I find a more satisfying, if less startling, summer in the passion of novelist and short-story writer Flannery O'Connor (1925–64). She was only 25 when her incurable lupus erythematosus was diagnosed. It was then that she returned to Georgia for good, able to write no more than two or three hours a day, but serenely aware that "vocation implies limitation." Several elements that were intrinsic to Flannery's vocation can, I believe, speak powerfully to today's Christians, especially in their midsummer.

First, Flannery wrote as she did because she was a Catholic. In many ways, a traditional Catholic. Her "center of existence" was the Eucharist; dogma did not fetter her but preserved mystery; faith gave her sufficient certainty to make her way "in darkness"; she could not meditate or contemplate, said prayers from the breviary, characterized her spirituality as "almost completely shut-mouth"; sin and grace were inescapably intertwined with human living; it was the Church that made the world endurable, and the Church was endurable because "it is somehow the body of Christ and on this we are fed."

Traditional yes, but not hidebound. "I am a Catholic peculiarly possessed of the modern consciousness, this thing Jung describes as unhistorical, solitary, and guilty. To possess this *within* the Church is to bear a burden, the necessary burden for the conscious Catholic. It's to feel the contemporary situation at the ultimate level." Flannery felt that "you have to suffer as much from the Church as for it," found smugness the great Catholic sin, was convinced that the conviction of the born Catholic, if severed from experience, made for harshness. As for the healing waters of Lourdes, she thought it easier to die for her religion "than take a bath for it." She could relate to a relative's attraction to the Church: "the sermons were so horrible, he knew there must be something else there to make the people come."

Second, Flannery was remarkably realistic. Perhaps the sheer uncertainty of tomorrow (she knew not the day nor the hour) made humbug uninviting—about herself, about her writing, and towards others. What could not be changed she accepted with serenity. Lupus "comes and goes, when it comes I retire and when it goes, I venture forth." She described her human and Christian struggle as "not struggle to submit but a struggle to accept and with passion. I mean, possibly, with joy." She felt that a friend's dissatisfaction with the Church might stem from an inadequate understanding of sin, from a demand "that the Church put the kingdom of heaven on earth right here now." Only bitterness could flower from such expectations. Sin being what it is and doing what it does, the Christian "knows how deep in you have to go to find love." A child can pick out faults in a Sunday sermon, but a child cannot possibly "find out the hidden love that makes a man, in spite of his intellectual limitations, his neuroticism, his own lack of strength, give up his life to the service of God's people, however bumblingly he may go about it."

To a friend, a Georgia writer, Flannery wrote that it wasn't any wonder he did not understand her novel *The Violent Bear It Away*, for he saw sex symbols everywhere. "I do hope that you will get over the kind of thinking that sees in every door handle a phallic symbol.... My Lord, Billy, recover your simplicity. You ain't in Manhattan. Don't inflict that stuff on the poor students there; they deserve better."

Third, Flannery's summer reveals a mature theology of suffering. It is strikingly summed up in her story "A Temple of the Holy Ghost." When a nun hugs a child, the crucifix on her belt is mashed into the side of the child's face, so that the accepted embrace is "marked with the ultimate all-inclusive symbol of love." The martyrdom the child "had thought about in a childish way (which turned into a happy sleeping with lions) is shown in the final way that it has to be for us all—an acceptance of the Crucifixion, Christ's and our own."

That is why Flannery could prefer to finish a novel than be able to walk again, even prayed at Lourdes for the novel she was working on, "not for my bones, which I care about less." That is why she could write to a specially dear, troubled, questing friend: "You will have found Christ when you are concerned with other people's sufferings and not your own." That is why she could confide to a perceptive admirer who would be close to her throughout her final illness: "I guess what you say about suffering being a shared experience with Christ is true, but then it should also be true of every experience that is not sinful. I mean that say, joy, may be a redemptive experience itself and not just the fruit of one. Perhaps however joy is the outgrowth of suffering in a special way."

Fourth, in almost 600 pages of correspondence there is not a single suggestion of self-pity. There is quiet humor: "I owe my existence and cheerful countenance to the pituitary glands of thousands of pigs butchered daily in Chicago Illinois at the Armour packing plant." There is what a friend called a "long love affair" with a flock of peafowl, Muscovy ducks, Chinese geese, and one-eyed swans. There is God—never far away, quietly loved, measured "by everything that I am not." And always there are people; for despite her need for creative solitude, she needed people, and people needed her. Flannery's last note, almost illegible, penned six days before her death, expressed concern for the safety of a friend.

I wish I had known her. There was so much Christlife in that frail frame . . . grace on crutches. The end of her life simply capped all that had gone before, could have had for epitaph the driving force she had revealed four years before:

"The human comes before art. You do not write the best you can for the sake of art but for the sake of returning your talent increased to the invisible God to use or not use as he sees fit." Amen.

AUTUMN

The years 40 to 45 spell transition. Early adulthood is ending, middle adulthood beginning. No single event has been found that proclaims this change for all everywhere, that heralds the autumn of life. Rather, a lived life is evolving. A man moves, Levinson's research reveals, from a season of "strength, quickness, endurance and output" to "a season when other qualities can ripen: wisdom, judiciousness, magnanimity, unsentimental compassion, breadth of perspective, the tragic sense." It may involve crisis, for youthful narcissistic pride has been wounded, insulted. "For large numbers of men, life in the middle years is a process of gradual or rapid stagnation, of alienation from the world and from the self." A man asks: Of what value is my life? Here, to struggle against stagnation is to struggle toward generativity—assuming responsibility for new generations of adults. It is the challenge of Jung's mid-life individuation, to acquire a clearer and fuller identity, to balance better the four psychological functions: thought, feeling, intuition, sensation.

Now Christian existence does not exempt us from the agonizing question: Is *my* life worth living? It can touch any mode or facet of existence: clerical consecration, religious vows, married life, job, church. . . . On our response and reaction depends our future: stagnation and alienation or clearer and fuller identity.

MY OWN AUTUMN

I was fortunate. During my passage to middle adulthood (the late 1950's) and through my early autumn a new world was struggling to birth, and the rural Woodstock where I hung my theological hat could not shelter me from it. The new man, the new woman, I met them everywhere—on street and campus, in sacristy and cocktail lounge, in the seminary classroom. John XXIII was opening storm windows; John Kennedy was coming with his Camelot; John Murray was uncovering a lost legacy of liberty. In its Christian dimension this new world was symbolized by a fresh vocabulary: charism, collegiality, community, conscience, dissent, ecumenism, experience, freedom, identity, integrity, peace, people of God, reconciliation, reform.

Very pertinently for me, priesthood was changing. When I offered my first Mass in '41, the ritual was highly stylized, quite solemn; my back was to the people, for the Eucharistic emphasis was exclusively on the high priest Christ. When I preached in the 40's and 50's, the sermon was a stepchild; the stress was so strongly on the sacrifice that you could miss the Word and not miss Mass. Ceaselessly I raised tired arms in absolution, for a sense of sin was pervasive. Believers besought me for solutions; and the solutions were given—clearly, objectively, with authority. Priesthood, like medicine and law, had status; some Catholics still tipped their hats as priests walked by, and thousands of young men felt called to priestly service. The prayer of priests was regular, regulated: breviary and meditation, thanksgiving after Mass and examination of conscience.

Back then we clergy were clean-shaven; hair dared not defile our ears. We wore the cassock—to the altar, to table, almost to bed; only on the golf course did we don the world's trousers. Rome expected us to be "out of this world," separated not only from evil but from much that is good; and in large measure we were. Friendships with women were discouraged; woman was indeed a soul to be saved, but a body to be shunned. Jesuits rose from sleep at 5:30 (our enemies said, 5:30 twice a day), and we were supposed to be home at a civilized hour.

Back then the priesthood may not have been paradise, but it was studded with stability and security; it was fenced about with fidelity. I could commit myself with confidence to a celibate existence for life, be respected for it, and expect to die in the warm arms of the Society of Jesus. We knew who we were, and it was good.

Change since John XXIII has cut the Church to its marrow. We have been torn within—from the kiss of peace through contraception to one true Church. Seminaries and convents have closed their doors; those that remain open seem to some all too open. The challenges to the priest—new demands and fresh expectations, unfamiliar freedoms and intolerable restrictions, dissatisfactions and resentments, low status and unrequited love, loneliness and a loss of identity (who am I?), a conviction that God is summoning to another way—these and a dozen other forces have decimated the clergy. In one ten-year period 10,000 American priests forsook the priesthood.

To the challenge of change I could hardly respond "no, thank you." Whether by God's grace or native stubbornness or middle-aged rut, I had no temptation whatever to be other than priest. But the underlying challenge remained: How react to a changing world, a changing Church, a changing priesthood? For me, it could not be simple acceptance or simple rejection. My problem was how to harmonize past and present, tradition and reform. I began to see that, like the Catholic Church or American society, I could preserve my identity, become I, only by adapting creatively to the new challenges.

A neat solution, but perilous. If, as historian John O'Malley put it, creativity "implies both utilization of the past and rejection of the past," if "the outcome of creativity is something *new*," I was in for a peck of trouble. I could no longer expect the past to *tell* me what to do. And yet the past was rooted in me—in my intelligence indeed, but more radically in my gut. My mind had fed on the Fathers of the Church, with their striking stress on tradition, summed up in the resounding affirmation that the norm of truth and true development is "what has been believed everywhere, always, by all." My philosophy, officially at least, was my seminary mélange of scholastics like Aquinas and Suárez. My spirituality was rooted in Ignatius Loyola and a thoroughly traditional, unvarying approach to his Spiritual Exercises. My asceticism was toughly negative, dominated by self-denial, putting to death the passions in my flesh. I do not regret these or reject them; but they had to ripen and expand, take on new colorations and fresh configurations. Otherwise I would be "out of this world."

But how do you balance thought, feeling, intuition, and sensation? Especially if, by genes and/or training, you are primarily a thinker, a weaver of words, a private person, untouched and untouching. How do you continue to discover God, sense His presence, in a world where the experience of God, encounter with God, the way God speaks, is radically different from yesterday? Where God is not nearly as accessible in the institutions and structures, the theologies and spiritualities that once mediated His presence, helped us to see His face? Where we are told, not by atheistic philosophers but by Christian theologians, that the God in whom we trusted is dead?

My own passage I have space to plot with broad strokes only. It did involve broadening the base of my experience: in philosophy (Whitehead, for one), in theology (the Lutheran-Catholic dialogue, for example), in spirituality (from Benedict to Merton), in actual living (more contact with the young, with the several faces of Eve). It meant challenging some basic presuppositions, or opening them up to challenge: on authority in the Church and the ministry of Protestants, on contraception and natural law, on sex and sexual sin, on loyalty to Rome and the freedom of the Christian conscience, on "one true Church." It made for agony and many a dark night of the soul. For over a decade, I was the only theologian in captivity acceptable to Rome (member of the papal International Theological Commission) and banned in Owensboro! And the struggle is not over, will never end this side of eternity; for what went into my fashioning in my Christian spring is difficult to root out, even to modify.

Several crucial episodes stand out. In the early 60's a young lady consulted me on a religious issue. As was my wont, I gave her *the* answer—with consummate clarity, impersonal objectivity, undoubted certitude. She looked at me a moment, then asked very simply: "And what do *you* think?" I gulped, visibly and audibly. I had always taken for granted that any answer I gave anyone was my answer. For the first time it struck me hammerlike, 't aint necessarily so. I did not realize it then, but I had touched a turning point. At 50.

Not long afterwards a friend asked compassionately: "Why are you so hard on yourself?" It was the only self-denial I knew:

keep that rebellious flesh under rigid control, and be intolerant of imperfection—mine and everyone else's! I suspect it can be traced back to several sources: the expectations of a strict father, the detailed demands and itemized prohibitions of earlier Catholic morality, a spirituality heavily freighted with "mortification," even a less than salutary fear of hell. Only in middle adulthood did I begin to approach what Jean Leclercq would call "an asceticism of humor." It involves the most difficult self-denial of all: you no longer take yourself too seriously. The days and nights no longer rotate around *you*, your heartache and your hiatal hernia, your problems and frustrations. You see yourself in perspective, as you really are, a creature wonderfully yet fearfully made, a bundle of paradoxes and contradictions. In brief, you can laugh at yourself *and* you put your trust in Another.

Liberating, too, was the growing realization (triggered largely by Jesuit seminarians at Woodstock in the steaming sixties) that I need not come to others with a hatful of answers, a sackful of solutions; they no longer believed I had them! I touch others most effectively when I come to them with my own brokenness. Not fearless and tearless, unscarred and unshaken. Like Christ, I am a *wounded* healer. I too am vulnerable; I too must confront the brutal condition of my mortality; ultimately I too stand alone before an abyss; I too must murmur "I believe, Lord; help my unbelief." It was a humbling and thrilling recognition: we are ministering, all of us, to one another, deepening our different pains to a level, a Calvary, where, in Henri Nouwen's words, "they can be shared as different manifestations of our similar dread-full condition."

What is to me of singular significance is that at 45, and more profoundly at 60, I could answer the question "Is my life worth living?" with a resounding and literal "By God, yes!" For each hour was lived more fully than in my summer, the more precious for being so precarious. Each friend, each person of the thousands I touched, seemed so much more real, came so incredibly alive. God's creation trailed wisps of God's glory: the blade of grass bending to the breeze, a single sparrow singing to the sun's new rising, the thunderous roar of His surf and the swift flash of His lightning. God Himself showed a different face, remarkably nearer; for I was not just knowing *about* Him, I was coming to know *Him*—not by the ladder of creatures, not through the symbols of theology, but as Gregory of Nyssa insisted: the best way to know God is to be like Him.

I had even begun to say "I." It is not easy if you have not been educated to it. Besides, there is a delicate line between the "I" that stirs others to think and tell their own story, and the "I" that embarrasses, that makes others mumble uncomfortably: "I'm sorry for your troubles, Father."

Still, I have come to resonate strongly to Carl Rogers' experience. This distinguished psychologist invariably found that the feeling which seemed to him most private and personal proved to be an expression for which there was a resonance in many another. It led him to the conviction that "what is most personal and unique in each one of us is probably the very element which would, if it were shared or expressed, speak most deeply to others." This helped him to "understand artists and poets as people who have dared to express the unique in themselves." Commenting on Rogers, Henri Nouwen suggested that "the Christian leader is first of all the artist who can bind together many people by his courage in giving expression to his most personal concern."

There was bitter anguish those middle years—from bouts with hypochondria and sin, through the sudden deaths of my dearest friends Gustave Weigel and John Courtney Murray and the lingering psychic dying of my mother, to the traumatic death of Woodstock College that had housed my head and my heart till I neared sixty. Ignatius Loyola, on his own admission, could have accepted in 15 minutes the destruction of his lifework, the Society of Jesus. It took me five or six years to come to terms with Woodstock's closing, to transcend the natural resentments, to fling away those unanswerable human questionings about right and wrong, wisdom or folly, to focus in my heart what I was preaching with my lips: only Jesus is indispensable, only Jesus is irreplaceable. "In no other name is there salvation save in the name of Jesus" (Acts 4:12).

Through all the middle-aged agonies there ran an abiding joy—yes, an occasional ecstasy. For our God is a God of understanding, who smiles gently over our foolishness; a God of fidelity, as faithful now to His fickle children as He was to early Israel; a God of love, who makes His presence felt when least we expect it. And so the autumn crises that shake you and shatter you can leave you with the experience of Peter, James, and John on the hill of transfiguration. You look up and you see no one—"no one but Jesus only" (Mt 17:8).

Again, my middle years are not a mirror in which many men and women can see their own lives. I have illustrated from my personal experience several significant conclusions reached by psychological research. The years 40 to 60 bring profound changes, some inevitable, others left to our choosing. They provoke a fearsome question: Of what value is my life? They may lead in either of two directions: to stagnation or to deeper identity.

MID-LIFE QUESTIONING

A powerful example of mid-life questioning is the remarkable author-monk Thomas Merton (1915–68). At 40, after 13 years with the Trappists, he had to ask himself: Should I leave? The factors that precipitated the crisis were several and varied. High on the list was the profound change in the monastery at Gethsemani in Kentucky. "The cloister," he had written five years before, "is as crowded as a Paris street. On the whole, when the house is completely full of men who are happy because they have not yet had a chance to suffer anything . . . the effect is a little disquieting. One feels more solidly rooted in God in a community of veterans, even though many of them may be morose." Communal life was putting him increasingly under tension. His old dream, to live as a hermit, tempted him ever more alluringly; he needed greater freedom for private prayer and contemplation.

But the official Visitor had roundly condemned the "hermit mentality" he found at Gethsemani, had specifically censured Merton for not being "in the mold" expected of a Trappist. Almost in desperation, Merton decided to ask Rome's Congregation for Religious to let him transfer to the Camaldolese, an Italian order of contemplatives who lived in a monastery but in nearly total solitude.

The problem was, his abbot did not want Merton to transfer. He foresaw serious scandal if this were to happen: scandal to Merton's students, who looked on him as an oracle of spirituality; scandal to other religious, who might become uneasy with their own way of life; scandal to his readers, who would see him as unstable. His influence as a writer would be markedly damaged; Trappist vocations would decline. In a letter to the distinguished Benedictine Jean Leclercq, the abbot described Merton as a neurotic, with poetic fancies and a love of adventure, not destined for solitary life, a man who would soon leave the Camaldolese as well. "Some new wild idea would hit him and off he would go. He would become a roamer, a gypsy."

Merton decided to submit, to stay. He would cease to write, at least for a while, would seek solitude only as it could be given in Gethsemani, as master of novices in the monastery's most secluded corner. "So I am grateful to God for fulfilling many of my desires when seeming to deny them. I know that I am closer to Him, and that all my struggles this year formed part of His plan. I am at peace in His will."

Not quite. Next year he was still depressed, decided he needed analysis, wrote for advice to the psychoanalyst Gregory Zilboorg. Without solitude or writing to relieve his tensions, his difficulty with superiors, he lived on the edge of a breakdown. He realized that all through his life a question confronts the monk with new meaning and urgency: What are you doing in the monastery? He found some help in the Virgin Mary's total submission to God's will (for the early monks, she was their "rule"). He came to feel that moving to another institution was not the solution. He consulted a psychiatrist, who concluded that Merton was one of the least neurotic persons in his experience, seriously misunderstood by his abbot. He found a part-time answer in a "hermitage" ten minutes from the abbey. Paradoxically, his inner conflict and Gethsemani's strict discipline were releasing him to a universe outside the monastery gates. Here, in part at least, was the springboard for his fresh activities in the 60's, his immersion in issues of peace and nuclear weapons, race and pollution. He was turning outward, involving himself in the sin and suffering of the world.

At 50 there was crisis again: how to live obedience when authority seems unreasonable; how to deal with the perils and pressures of solitude; how to harmonize his hermit side with his need for people and their need for him. He had problems with "where is the Church and where am I in the Church?" He had to argue passionately, at times angrily, with theologian Rosemary Radford Ruether, who charged that in his monastic life he had "withdrawn from creation into hell." He had to admit to her his deep fears that his life might be a lie, and yet his conviction that he was right to stay where he was.

The cost, now as before, was high: stomach spasms, colitis, tensions that tied his "guts in knots of utter despair." No wonder he could write wittily to a troubled friend: "You think I got fun here? Man, you think more. You think I got no angst? Man, think again. I got angst up to the eyes."

These middle years of Merton have been appraised in startlingly different ways. Biographer Monica Furlong concludes that in this period of crises Merton changed enormously. He was no longer the pious monk blindly trusting authority. He was questioning: the structure of Gethsemani life, its mechanization and modernization, the boredom and lifelessness of much monastic labor, the "overcontrol" of the monks. His awareness of change coming upon his Church and his order "coincided for him with an extraordinary inner development." He thirsted once again for literature on a strikingly wide scale—e.g., novelists and dramatists, poetry and politics, psychology and theology—not for orthodoxy or piety but with one overriding question: Could they tell him something about the contemporary world? These years help mightily to persuade Furlong that Merton chose badly when he decided to become a Trappist; some other order would have proved more congenial to his gifts and his temperament.

Fellow monk John Eudes Bamberger, a student, avid disciple, and spiritual advisee of Merton during some of those tempestuous years, finds it misleading to present Merton's development as progressive "alienation from an essentially uncongenial monastic environment and superior." Two months before his death he wrote from Calcutta to his supposedly unsympathetic abbot: "Our different views certainly did not affect our deep agreement on the real point of life and of our vocation." A month later he confided to his *Asian Journal* that "the lack of quiet and the general turbulence" at Gethsemani were indications that he "ought to move." But "would this move be *temporary or permanent?* I do not think I ought to separate myself completely from Gethsemani. . . . I suppose I ought eventually to end my days there. I do in many ways miss it. There is no problem of my wanting simply to 'leave Gethsemani.' It is my monastery, and being away has helped me to see it in perspective and love it more."

Indeed, Bamberger grants, there were periods of severe trial "that caught Merton at some of his weak points." He did become confused, had to struggle with the life of a hermit, slipped in fidelity awhile; there were "very real shadows and doubts, those that were well-founded and those that came from his own weaknesses." And still "he was a very humble and consistently obedient monk" who in the end repudiated the behavior of those critical years. He had to grow into maturity as a Cistercian, as a monk of Gethsemani; and he did.

When Merton died so tragically and so young—accidentally electrocuted in Bangkok at 53—he was still looking for deeper and deeper identity. In a decade he had changed much, discovered much. Illusions about religious life had been stripped away. He had gone through the loneliness of the desert, lost his way, found a more profound self that pervaded his final years.

Six days before his death, Merton had the most remarkable experience of his Asian pilgrimage, at Polonnaruwa in Ceylon, where he approached the Buddhas "barefoot and undisturbed, my feet in wet grass, wet sand." As he looked at the silent, smiling, subtle faces, an inner clarity seemed to explode from the rocks. "I know and have seen what I was obscurely looking for. I don't know what else remains but I have now seen and have pierced through the surface and have got beyond the shadow and the disguise."

Yes, mid-life often calls for a conversion. Not simply the ceaseless conversion that is inseparable from Christian living, the endless turning to Christ that should dawn afresh with each day. For many, a more radical conversion: if I am not to stagnate, I must turn my life around. Precisely how I turn, where, to what—God, work, or people; church or family; desert or city—this will vary, depending on who I am, where I've been, where I'm at. But turn I must, else I die. Not physical death. Far worse: I deaden the image of God in me.

Despite the inevitable agony in radical conversion, it can be, should be, instinct with joy. Andrew Greeley phrased it strikingly in *The Mary Myth:* "Falling in love again, we are told by those who have done it, is much more fun than the first time around. Similarly, being born again was a much greater adventure for the human race than being born for the first time."

TRAPPED

Very touching, even poetic and romantic; but how do you turn your life around if you're trapped? Some men and women are trapped from within, by their own psyches. I remember, with affection and sadness, that incomparable actor Peter Sellers. This "prime minister of mirth," as *Time* dubbed him at his death, was alive only when he was impersonating, playing to perfection the role of another: a German scientist or an R.A.F. officer, president of the U.S. or Cockney Marxist, an Indian doctor or a bumbling French detective, a dowager and her friends. Offscreen he may well have been the simple-minded gardener he plays in *Being There,* victim of a corporate state that through TV "has rendered him unaware, passive, with no notion of himself, his own life, or of others." Sellers was rootless, changing residences like clothes; 70 cars in six years; four marriages; few relationships that were lasting or intimate. And "when the world closed in, he sought refuge variously in women, yoga, vegetarianism and overwork."

At times, fortunately, the scenario ends more happily; the actor emerges from the prison of his psyche. I've just finished

Sid Caesar's own story. Sid was surely one of America's premier comedians. At mid-century Alfred Hitchcock said that Sid "best approaches the great Chaplin of the early 1920's." And yet, from early adulthood and on through thirty-four years he was increasingly tortured by guilt and fear. Guilt over all sorts of things: for being so ungrateful, for special treatment in military service, for making much more money than his father, for undeserved success. Fear of failing, of not measuring up, of rejection real or imagined; afraid that all this had come too fast, too easily. He was basically a loner, terribly shy, with no self-esteem. But, for good or ill, there was always someone to keep him from falling utterly apart: father, wife, colleagues.

And so, highly successful, making $4000 a week at 32, Sid Caesar drank to oblivion, took pills with his liquor, ate his gluttonous way to 240 pounds, was forever throwing up. He was an aggressive, destructive drunk who cast chairs into a swimming pool and came close to throwing friend Mel Brooks out of an eighteenth-story window in Chicago.

Psychiatry over five years had little effect. He would not go to Alcoholics Anonymous lest his secret leak out. He felt he had to keep punishing himself, would not let himself be happy. Irrationally, he envied others' success. He took out his frustrations on a devoted wife, was devastatingly sarcastic to his children. He forced friends to defect, challenged executives to see him as an oaf so that they would not hire him.

Sid's mid-fifties were the darkest of his dark period. For four months in 1978 he never left the house, hardly ever got out of bed, lived off liquor and pills, constantly thought of suicide. But on May 22nd of that year, on an opening night in Regina, Saskatchewan, the great depression bottomed out. He begged a hotel doctor: "Help me . . . please help me."

The painful road back moved from health of body to health of mind. Five months in Paris were crucial: a constant conversation, on cassettes, between Sid the parent and Sidney the wayward child. It was akin to Jungian spontaneous analysis. Opening up about loneliness and anger, about guilt and un-worthiness. Dialogue with that part of himself which was the source of his anger and pain, and coming to terms with it. Making friends with himself.

On December 12, 1980 Sid discovered that he was impor-tant to *himself*—and that's what counts. It helped reverse a fearful childhood memory: his ten-year-old brother letting in-fant Sid's carriage roll downhill, only an unseen rope stopping it at the bottom. His own hands were now on the carriage; *he* was in control.

For such as Sellers and Caesar, the psyche is a dread cap-tor. Others are trapped from the outside, by the situation or circumstances in which they find themselves. Take work, for example. For millions of men and women, work is an imper-sonal assembly line; the end product is rarely their creation; what they make is expected to break down; the emphasis is, how much money in how few hours; the sense of vocation is dead. And to change the system is to rend society's fabric. Lit-tle wonder a workingwoman has remarked: "Most of us, like the assembly-line worker, have jobs that are too small for our spirit. Jobs are not big enough for people."

Eight hours of monotonous toil; eight more hours of sleep to do that work; what is left? Is only one third of your life alive? And what manner of man, what kind of woman, will you be at 65? Is your work, as one such slave phrased it, "a drain down which I'm pouring my life"?

Enslaving work frays not only the blue collar. For many in the middle years, the joy has disappeared from medicine or the law, from the executive desk, the drawing board, the class-room. Even if the excitement and the challenge remain, too of-ten the price is excessive: your very success involves a subtly dehumanizing life style, a type of house in a kind of setting with a coterie of friends you have not freely chosen, imposed on you by your job, with no option other than to surrender the specialty in which you delight or settle for an end to ambition. Not infrequently, the need to succeed drains the love out of a home.

This is not the place to resolve such complex conflicts in society and the home. But if the medieval mystic Meister Eckhart was right when he wrote, "Wisdom consists in doing the next thing you have to do, doing it with your whole heart, and finding delight in doing it," then many, if not most, middle-age Americans are experiencing in their work a crisis of wisdom. Not because they have deliberately chosen to be foolish. Often the rut could not have been foreseen; where it could, or was, all too often options were closed by circumstances, relationships, obligations, limited competences. It is relatively easy for a vowed religious to bid good-by to a destructive routine: the vineyards are many and varied, superiors are normally open to persuasive argument (or to intractable stubbornness), and I do not have a family to support. The laity are rarely so fortunate.

I have discovered no miracle drug. I have experienced, however, that husbands and wives are more likely to survive the threat of stagnation, to acquire a clearer and fuller identity, if they are able to communicate, to share their disappointments and frustrations, their pain and distress, their bitterness, their sense of inadequacy; if over the years they have grown together in intimacy with Christ and sensitivity to *his* cross in their lives; if they are not locked into a single, imprisoning way of life, but are genuinely, prayerfully open to fresh whisperings of the Spirit. These are not solutions to concrete problems; they are human and Christian attitudes that lie at the root of change, of conversion, of adaptation.

NEED FOR A SPIRITUALITY

Here I am suggesting that, for those who believe, a creative response to mid-life crises calls for a spirituality, a loving
relationship with a living Lord within a community. Prefera-
bly, not a spirituality that has to be invented on your forty-fift
birthday; rather, one that has evolved and deepened throug
four decades. Let me simply sketch a few facets of such a spi
tuality that reflect my own experiences—experiences so lo
delayed that I echo Augustine's "Late have I loved thee."

First, a basic truth: each of us is called to be holy. ""
must be perfect as your heavenly Father is perfect" (Mt 5:4
not a summons to a privileged few. In our very baptism
the dying-rising Christ we are all summoned to a life we
takenly reserve to Francis of Assisi, Teresa of Avila, or I
Pio. I mean the mystical life. But mystical life in the sense
Gerson gave it in the Middle Ages: knowledge of God by
rience, arrived at through the embrace of unifying love
should not be an extraordinary experience; certainly it
miraculous. If the word "mystical" makes you uneasy,
aside. You are called to a loving experience of God. It
God gives to those who open themselves to Him alr
home within them.

The obstacle, of course, is "the daily grind." Whet
law office in Washington or a refugee road out of Leba
house full of jet-propelled children, "the embrace of
love" gets lost in brutal reality. And yet without holi
is no Christian solution, at times no human solution,
crises. It may be that here the experience of the gre
is instructive: most fruitful for oneness with God has
constant meditation on the passion of Christ.

Second, a cultural obstruction: the Western m
generation have been head worshipers. For us,
peak of knowledge is Descartes's clear and disti

consequence, we rarely live in awareness of our fuller selves. We are not in ceaseless touch with our senses; we bury our feelings; we find fantasy unreal, relegate imagination to the edge of our existence, to times of relaxation. This is not just a deficiency on the level of the sheerly human. It makes prayer burdensome, an exercise in ideas, abstract thought, discursive analysis. It keeps me from feeling the touch of God, experiencing God in the sensations of my hand, in different parts of my body. Without such awareness of the divine, my prayer will prove to be a wedding of reason and voice, at best a loud cry of petition to a Lord somewhere out there. No, the rock bottom of a living spirituality is a God who touches me, a God I feel.

Third, a Catholic spirituality must have its center in the Eucharist. For the Eucharist, as Monika Hellwig insists, "is the center of all we do and are and hope as Christians." But is it? Does my Eucharistic sharing in the death and resurrection of Jesus so transform me that my focus shifts from myself to the needs of others, from a siege or bomb-shelter mentality to a struggle against the barriers that divide? If I am to be a eucharist for the life of the world, my feeding on the flesh of Christ must take me from church to world, must fashion my own "real presence." I must begin to be present to others, present where they are, present in ways that respond to their hungers—for food or freedom, for peace or truth, for understanding or God. I must be really present—I, not merely my money or my mind—somewhat hidden at times but always totally committed, because as a Christian my life is love and only love can bring life, can light dulled eyes with hope, can promise somebody somewhere that tomorrow will be more human, will be worth living.

Such transformation (and this is but one way of looking at the Eucharist) can help prevent the stagnation that threatens mid-life. It can lend fresh purpose to an existence that centers in self, work that only frustrates, religion that is rote, love that

has cooled. But it will not happen if the central act of our faith, the paschal mystery, has itself turned into just another obligation, a ritual I attend, an hour I endure.

Just as urgently, a Eucharistic spirituality must focus on community. The Bread of Life is not primarily an individualistic thing, a solitary supper, my private party. St. Paul phrased it beautifully: "Because the Bread is one, we, though many, are one body; for we all partake of the one Bread" (1 Cor 10:17). The Lord who locks himself in the tabernacle of my body is none other than the Lord who nourishes my next-door neighbor, the same Christ who feeds the Lebanese, the Japanese, and the Thai, the African, the German, and the Czech. Christ is not divided, Christ is not multiplied. There is one and the same body, one and the same Christ, for all. In his flesh we are one.

A peril for Catholic spirituality today is that the Eucharist which should make us one threatens to divide us. Catholic communities are unchristianly rent by warring loves. Shall we stand or kneel, pray in an ageless Latin or an ephemeral English, receive Life in our hands or on our tongues, wish peace with a touch or a word, blare forth Bach from an organ or strum a Christian love song? For all too many, these are life-and-death struggles—so much so that some Catholics will not worship with other Catholics save on their own narrow terms, even suicidally refuse the Bread that gives life. Is it for this that the Word-made-flesh offered that flesh the night before he died: "This is my body, which is given for you"?

Fourth, a Catholic spirituality recognizes, and lives with, what an imaginative fellow Jesuit, William Lynch, called "the structure of ugliness and eternal beauty, not the second on the outside of the first, but the two tightly interpenetrating each other." That twin structure is found both in Christ and in his Church. There is the Isaian Christ in whom "there is no comeliness and no beauty" (Isa 53:2), and there is the Christ of the

Song of Songs, "the radiant and ruddy lover" (Cant 5:10). Not two persons; no, one and the same, the dying-rising Christ. The same interpenetration of scandal and glory, Father Lynch notes, is to be found in the Church. On the one hand, you can hear Christ, as some Fathers of the Church did, addressing his beloved, the Church he has wed to himself with his blood:

> Ah, you are beautiful, my love,
>   ah, you are beautiful!
> Your eyes are doves
>   behind your veil.
> Your hair is like a flock of goats,
>   moving down the slopes of Gilead.
> Your teeth are like a flock of shorn ewes
>   that have come up from the washing,
> all of which bear twins,
>   and not one among them is bereaved.
> Your lips are like a scarlet thread,
>   and your mouth is lovely.
> Your cheeks are like halves of a pomegranate
>   behind your veil.
> Your neck is like the tower of David,
>   built for an arsenal,
> whereon hang a thousand bucklers,
>   all of them shields of warriors.
> Your two breasts are like two fawns,
>   twins of a gazelle,
>   that feed among the lilies. . . .
> You are all fair, my love;
>   there is no flaw in you.
>
> (Cant 4: 1–5, 7)

On the other hand, this same Church which Christ "cleansed by the washing of water with the word, that he might present [her] to himself in splendor, without spot or wrinkle or any such thing, that she might be holy and without blemish" (Eph 5:26–27), has a shockingly human face. As an expressive symbol of this, Lynch quotes a graphic paragraph from George Bernard Shaw:

> In Italy, for instance, churches are used in such a way that priceless pictures become smeared with filthy tallowsoot, and have sometimes to be rescued by the temporal power and placed in national galleries. But worse than this are the innumerable daily services which disturb the truly religious visitor. If these were decently and intelligently conducted by genuine mystics to whom the mass was no mere rite or miracle, but a real communion, the celebrants might reasonably claim a place in the church as their share of the common human right to its use. But the average Italian priest, personally uncleanly, and with chronic catarrh of the nose and throat, produced and maintained by sleeping and living in frowsy, ill-ventilated rooms, punctuating his gabbled Latin only by expectorative hawking, and making the decent guest sicken and shiver every time the horrible splash of spitten mucus echoes along the vaulting from the marble steps of the altar: this unseemly wretch should be seized and put out, bell, book, candle, and all, until he learns to behave himself.

Sorry, Mr. Shaw. It is no aseptic body of Christ to which we belong—no more aseptic than "the parts of the body which seem to be weaker ... and those parts of the body which we think less honorable" (1 Cor 12:22–23). A church "for saints only" was a fourth-century heresy. Sinners, like the poor, we have with us always. Not only *with* us. To each of us a just God can say what the prophet Nathan said to the adulterous murderer King David: "*You* are the man" (2 Sam 12:7). It reminds me of a moving meditation in which French Jesuit (now Cardinal) Henri de Lubac, much maligned over the so-called New Theology of the late 40's, has expressed the paradox of a

Church whose features are a "wedding of opposites." In part he writes:

> I am told that she is holy, yet I see her full of sinners. I am told that her mission is to tear man away from his earthly cares, to remind him of his eternal vocation, yet I see her constantly preoccupied with the things of the earth and of time, as if she wished us to live here forever. I am assured that she is universal, as open as divine intelligence and charity, and yet I notice very often that her members, through some sort of necessity, huddle together timidly in closed groups—as human beings do everywhere. She is hailed as immutable, alone stable and above the whirlpools of history, and then, suddenly, under our very eyes, she upsets many of the faithful by the suddenness of her renewals. . . .
>
> She is both human and divine, given from above, and come from below. Those who belong to her resist, with all the weight of a burdened and wounded nature, the Life with which she tries to permeate them. She is turned toward the past, meditating on a memorial which she knows contains what will never be surpassed; and, at the same time, she looks to the future and rejoices in the hope of an ineffable fulfillment that suffers not even a glimpse. Called, in her present form, to disappear completely from the face of this world, she is destined, in her very essence, to remain whole from the day her innermost being is disclosed. Varied and multiform, she is nonetheless one with the most active and the most demanding unity. She is a people, a huge anonymous crowd, and yet—what other expression is there—the most personal Being. Catholic, that is, universal, she wants her members to be open to all, yet she is only fully herself when she withdraws to the intimacy of her interior life in the silence of adoration. She is both humble and majestic. She claims to assimilate every culture and ennoble its every value; at the same time, she sees herself the home of little ones, the poor, the simple, miserable multitude. Not for a moment does she pause—for this would mean her death, and she is immortal—in contemplating him who is at once the crucified and the resurrected, the Man of suffering and the Lord of

glory, the Victim of the world and its Savior, at once her
bleeding Spouse and her triumphant Master, the Heart wide-
open and ever infinitely secret, from whom she received her
existence, from whom she draws at every moment of her history the Life she yearns to share with all.

It is this paradox of the divine and human intertwined in
the Church that my spirituality must reflect. Else it risks being
less than Christian, because less reflective of Christ. In de Lubac's fertile phrase, "The whole Church passes into a saint."

This leads quite naturally to a fifth facet of Catholic spirituality that bears on mid-life crises: the centrality of the cross.
But let me postpone this to my final season, when I shall come
to speak of the suffering that attends our human wintering.
For the present, I simply suggest that a spirituality not intimately nailed to Calvary is a Christian mirage. Since it does
not stem from the source of genuinely Christian living, the dying-rising Christ, it can hardly help the Christian in his or her
constant movement between death and resurrection.

Here I recall how Teilhard de Chardin discovered in attachment and detachment the two phases of life's basic
rhythm. To be myself, I must develop myself; to be in another,
I must surrender to diminishment. And the paradigm, the pattern, of Christian attachment and detachment is the crucified
Christ.

I am not asserting that the struggle against stagnation, the
effort to acquire a fuller identity, is impossible apart from
Christ (though I suspect we have not yet plumbed the early
Christian conviction that with the Incarnation the *whole* of
created reality has taken on a fresh texture, a new vesture).
Uncounted individuals from Aristotle through Mohammed to
Sid Caesar have "made it" by ways and means that have no
palpable link to the God-man. But I am a Christian speaking in
the first instance to Christians, to men and women who at

some time or other have confessed that only Jesus is *their* Savior. For such as these, for such as me, an integral component of mid-life wholeness is such selfless love as once inspired a famous sonnet long attributed to the heroic sixteenth-century missionary St. Francis Xavier. It is not really his, but it is expressive of his love. This Spanish sonnet loses something in my translation, but the basic idea breaks through:

> It is not your promised heaven
> That moves me, Lord, to love you.
> It is not the fear of hell
> That forces me to fear you.
>
> What moves me, Lord, is you, Lord,
> Fixed to a cross and mocked.
> What moves me is your wounded body,
> The insults and your death.
>
> What moves me really is your love, so that
> Were there no heaven, I would love you still,
> Were there no hell, I would fear you still.
> For me to love you, you need nothing give,
> For even if I did not hope as indeed I hope,
> Even so I would love you as indeed I love.

WINTER

At about 60 the male of the species faces a new transition: to late adulthood. I am powerfully reminded that I am moving from middle age to a generation for which we have only a frightening term: old age. For perhaps the first time I experience mortality. Oh, I always *knew* I was mortal; now I sense it. Soldiers feel it in a foxhole; I feel it in my flesh.

The decline, experts insist, actually began at 30, but now it is transparent. Joints ache, a virus will not leave me, ligaments heal slowly. Cucumbers make me throw up, and sauerkraut makes for diarrhea. For some there is a stroke, a growth, a clot. No matter what, I am not what I was. This flesh that gloried in its strength, that lusted in its manhood, that tanned so evenly, is wasting. Once a week the bell tolls for someone I know. And I'm afraid that maybe, like my mother, I will lose my memory, my arteries will harden, senility will set in.

At this stage I must face up to Erikson's key polarity: integration versus despair. Somehow I must grasp my life as something whole. Only then can I live late adulthood, old age, without bitterness or despair; only thus can I come to terms with death. It means I am aware of my lack of wholeness, of my corruption; I make peace with my flawed existence. And to continue creative, I must retain my link to youthful vitality, my tie to the forces of growth in myself and in the world. Otherwise this will prove only the winter of my discontent.

INTEGRATION VERSUS DESPAIR

But how do this, how grasp my life as something whole? The problem is complicated by an ideal—the ideal of old age that America has fashioned. We inhabit a culture that canonizes youth and beauty, activity and productivity, power and sexual prowess. If you are eternally young and ceaselessly attractive, if after 60 or 65 you continue your career with little letdown and still make an impact on an acre of God's world, if you can jog or play squash or straddle a Honda, if you can still satisfy a man or woman sexually, then your aging is ideal. In fact, you're not growing old at all! The ideal is a compound of Churchill and John XXIII, Picasso and Susan B. Anthony, Maurice Chevalier and Marlene Dietrich, George Meany and Mae West, George Burns and Lauren Bacall, Clark Gable and Grandma Moses. The only ideal of old age we accept in America is an old age without change or limits or loss.

If this be ideal old age, it is a tragic ideal; for it is not our ordinary experience. Only a very few continue their careers after 65; only a very few live the dominant ideal. In *The Coming of Age* Simone de Beauvoir put it painfully well:

> Apart from some exceptions, the old man no longer *does* anything. He is defined by an *exis*, not by a *praxis*: a being, not a

doing. Time is carrying him towards an end—death—which
is not *his* and which is not postulated or laid down by any
project. This is why he looks to active members of the community like one of a 'different species', one in whom they do
not recognize themselves.

An ideal that can be lived only by the rich, the talented, the
powerful is hardly a viable ideal.

Basic to a Christian theology for the aging is a sacred
Christian symbol: kenosis. The Greek word means an "empty-
ing." The archetype of emptying, in the Christian tradition, is
Christ Jesus, who, in St. Paul's powerful phrasing,

> though of divine status,
> did not treat like a miser's booty
> his right to be like God
> [his right to appear like Yahweh in glory],
> but emptied himself of it,
> to take up the status of a slave
> and become like men.
> Having assumed human form,
> he still further humbled himself
> with an obedience that meant death—
> even death upon a cross!
>
> (Phil 2:5–8)

This archetypal emptying finds a moving analogue in the Gospel scene where the risen Jesus addresses Peter, who has thrice
protested that he does indeed love his Lord: "Truly, I assure
you, when you were a young man, you used to fasten your own
belt and set off for wherever you wished. But when you grow
old, you will stretch out your hands, and another will fasten a
belt around you and take you where you do not wish to go" (Jn
21:18).

I am not suggesting that Jesus was lecturing Peter on ger-
ontology. Still, the scene is provocative for our problem. In the
Catholic vision, aging calls for a kenosis which radically sun-

ders old age from youth, an emptying which can rarely be denied, a progressive loss which must be faced, evaluated, transcended. Of course age diminishes me. How could it not?

The point is, aging need not be an enemy. The Christian Scriptures will not accept the more classical idea that adult maturity is a finished state, that at a certain point, at the peak of physical and intellectual manhood or womanhood, you are the complete person, you have it made, you have reached perfection. No, life is an endless pilgrimage; the Christian is a pilgrim, a wayfarer. The perfection of a Christian man or woman is total conformity to the humanness of Christ—and that is a ceaseless process, never achieved here below.

Essential to the pilgrimage is kenosis: you have to let go. From the very shape of the human journey. For the journey to go forward, to move ahead, you have to let go of where you've been, let go of the level of life where you are now, so as to live more fully. Whether it's turning 21, 40, or 65; whether it's losing your health or your hair, your looks or your lustiness, your money or your memory, a person you love or a possession you prize; whether it's yesterday's applause or today's rapture; whether it's as fleeting as Malibu's surf or as abiding as God's grace—you have to move on. Essential to the human pilgrimage, to the Christian journey, is a self-emptying more or less like Christ's own emptying: time and again, from womb to tomb, you have to let go. And to let go is to die a little. It's painful, it can be bloody; and so we hang on, we clutch our yesterdays like Linus' blanket, we refuse to grow.

That refusal to grow, to let go, I find powerfully symbolized in an old movie, *Come Back, Little Sheba*. The male lead, Burt Lancaster, is a reformed alcoholic. His wife, Shirley Booth, is a devoted woman with a big heart; but she bores him endlessly by ceaselessly recalling the good old days. Remember when . . . ? Time and again she walks out on the porch calling for Little Sheba, the dog that has disappeared, the dog that is a symbol of those bygone days, a symbol of dashed hopes. And for twenty years these two good people live what Thoreau called "lives of quiet desperation."

But what is it I am growing into? Here I might well be mute, did not faith give me tongue. But not quite. Believer and unbeliever alike can grow into love. A quieter love, of course, without the passion of yesterday; but surely richer, perhaps deeper, because mellowed by every face I've seen or touched, softened from the anger and fear of yesteryear, grown more understanding of difference and diversity, more tolerant of the sinner in all of us. A love that has learned to listen. A love that at long last "is patient and kind, is not jealous or boastful, is not arrogant or rude, does not insist on its own way, is not irritable or resentful, does not rejoice at wrong but rejoices in the right" (1 Cor 13:4–6).

And yet, it is my Christian faith that concretizes this love. As a Christian, my burden and my glory is to grow into Christ. Kenosis is not its own end. The Christian lets go because only by letting go does he or she grow gradually into Christ, come to be conformed to his life and death, fashioned to his passion and resurrection. It is in this way that the Christian reaches oneness, not with abstract transcendence but with Someone Transcendent, with the triune personal Love we call God. Self-realization through self-transcendence.

The point is: for the Christian, life, eternal life, eternal life granted already on this earth, "consists in this," as Jesus said to his Father the night before he died, "that they know you, the one true God, and the one whom you sent, Jesus Christ" (Jn 17:3). Not a purely intellectual affair. Here, to "know" connotes immediate experience and intimacy; it involves a loving communion with God, with His human images on earth, with every work of His hands. It is this loving communion that I am committed to grow into.

There should be a kenosis, an emptying, a letting go, all

through human living; but aging and the losses of aging press kenosis to its nadir, its low point. Loss is heaped on loss, indignity on indignity—social and psychic, physical and intellectual—to the ultimate indignity that is death. Like Christ, I am stripped naked, for all the world to see—if it cares to look. What is left is not what I have achieved, not what I have amassed; what is left is who I am. It can be a frightening relic, a soul-shattering image; but there I am, at this stage of the pilgrimage. There am I, there is God, there are "the others." Do I "know" them?

CONTEMPLATION

But if the purpose of kenosis is to transcend self, to come into loving communion with Someone Transcendent and with His created reflections, how is this achieved? After four decades of searching, my response is: through contemplation. Oh, not the popular sense of "contemplate," which all too many instantly associate with "navel." Contemplation in its profound sense is something just as real as your navel but immeasurably more exciting. My Carmelite friend William McNamara—a contemplative whose spoken word is fused of fire and softness, who sparkles with Isaian woe and Irish wit—once called contemplation "a pure intuition of being, born of love. It is experiential awareness of reality and a way of entering into immediate communion with reality. Reality? Why, that means people, trees, lakes, mountains.... You can study things, but unless you enter into this intuitive communion with them, you can only know *about* them, you don't *know* them. To take a long loving look at something—a child, a glass of wine, a beautiful meal—this is a natural act of contemplation, of loving admiration.... To be able to do that, there's the rub. All the way through school we are taught to abstract; we are not taught loving awareness."

Never have I heard contemplation more engagingly defined: a long loving look at the real. Each word is crucial: the real . . . look . . . long . . . loving. The "real" here is not some far-off, abstract, intangible God-in-the-sky. Reality is living, pulsing people; reality is fire and water; reality is the sun setting over the Poconos and a gentle doe streaking through the forest; reality is a ruddy glass of Burgundy, Beethoven's Mass in D, a child lapping a chocolate ice-cream cone; reality is a striding woman with wind-blown hair; reality is Christ Jesus. Paradoxically, the one thing excluded from contemplation is the one thing we identify with it: abstraction—where a leaf is no longer green, water no longer ripples, a woman is no longer soft, and God no longer smiles. What I contemplate is always what is most real: what philosophers call the concrete singular.

This real I "look" at. I no longer analyze it or argue it, describe or define it; I am one with it. I do not move around it; I enter into it. Remember Eric Gill's outraged protest? "Good Lord! The thing was a mystery and we measured it!" Walter Kerr, in his delightful book *The Decline of Pleasure*, compared contemplation to falling in love:

> To fall in love with someone is, in a real but maddeningly inarticulate way, to know someone. . . . [But] not . . . in terms of its height, weight, coloring, ancestry, intellectual quotient, or acquired habits. . . . A person who is "known" is known *through* these qualities but never simply by them. . . . No one of these things—not all of them together—precisely identifies the single, simple vibration that gives us such joy in the meeting of eyes or the lucky conjunction of interchanged words. Something private and singular and uniquely itself is touched—and known in the touching.

In contemplation, I simply "see."

This look at the real is a "long" look. Not in terms of measured time, but wonderfully unhurried, gloriously unharried. For Americans, time is a stop watch, time is money; life is a race against time. To contemplate is to rest—to rest in the real. Not lifelessly or languidly, not sluggishly or inertly. My whole being is alive, incredibly responsive, vibrating to every throb of the real. For once, time is irrelevant. You do not time Eugene Ormandy and the Philadelphia Symphony; you do not clock the Last Supper. I am reminded of the Louvre in Paris and the haunting Mona Lisa. I recall an endless line of tourists, ten seconds each without ever stopping; over against that, a lone young man on a stone bench, eyes riveted, whole person enraptured, sensible only to beauty and mystery, aware only of the real.

But this long look at the real must be a "loving" look. It is not a fixed stare, not the long look of a Judas. To be one with the real means to love the real. It demands that the real delight me, captivate me. Tchaikovsky's *Swan Lake Ballet* or lobster cardinal, the grace of a woman's walk or the compassion in the eyes of Christ—whatever or whoever the real, contemplation calls forth love, pleasure, delight. For contemplation is not study, is not cold examination; contemplation is not a computer. To contemplate is to be in love—with the things of God, with the people of God, with God Himself.

A long loving look at the real—this alone is contemplation. It is seeing things as they really are. It is the biblical "Be still, and know that I am God" (Ps 46:10). It is St. Teresa of Avila gorging on a roast partridge. The nuns are scandalized. Teresa laughs: "At prayer time, pray! At partridge time, partridge!" That is why Kazantzakis loved her so lustily. From such contemplation comes pure pleasure, the pleasure modern man resists because it is "useless." From such contemplation comes communion. I mean the discovery of the Holy in profound human encounters, where love is proven by sacrifice, the wild exchange of all else for God. Thus is fashioned what the second-century bishop Irenaeus called "God's glory—man/woman alive!"

Is this "for real"? Am I seriously submitting that a cultural model for the aging is discoverable in contemplation? In one word, yes. In our passion for doing, we have forgotten or betrayed an ageless tradition that transcends cultures, that permeates not only the Hebrew Testament and the life of Jesus but the Platonists and Aristotle, the Stoics and Plotinus, not only the desert fathers of early Christianity and the medieval mystics but the daily life of India and Islam.

Oh, I know, contemplation as a model for the aging confronts obvious obstacles. First, it clashes with our culture; it runs counter to a twentieth-century American article of faith: only useful activity is valuable. If you are not active, you are not alive. Second, the model meets resistance in the real: most of the aging are anxious, are concerned about sheer survival, how to pay for today, how to cope with arthritic joints and tumorous flesh; it is so hard to "rest" in the real. Third, we are not educated to contemplation; we have not been taught loving awareness. At sixty-five it is not easy to *begin* looking long and lovingly at the real; it is easier to start jogging.

And still it *must* come to pass. Without contemplation we will continue to find or create "things to be done" as therapy for enforced idleness, a therapy that makes the old into second-class citizens on the edge of human living. Without contemplation the people will perish; for aging will be meaningless, Macbeth's "tale told by an idiot, full of sound and fury, signifying nothing." But with contemplation the aging can afford to let go, to be emptied, because kenosis is recognized as the way to living in the present, receiving this moment as a gift rich in its possibilities. With contemplation I do not merely remember an irretrievable past, mourn each autumn leaf that falls. All that has gone is gathered together, comes to focus, to a still point, in my now. With contemplation old age can be growth as well as decline, a time of increased innerness. I am no longer what I do; I am who I am. With contemplation suffering need not be painful waste; the Christian can transform it into sacrifice, by making it an expression of love, a sharing in the Christ whose self-giving was redemptive. With contemplation I can crystallize my Christian conviction that God cares. Even loveless and alone, I am loved.

But how realize this capacity for contemplation? Four practical (or impractical) suggestions. First, as William McNamara never tires of repeating, some sort of desert experience. Not necessarily the physical desert of the Bible, the proving ground of Jesus and the desert fathers. The process can be initiated by any experience—old age itself—that brings you face to face with solitude, with vastness, with powers of life and death beyond your control, with your vulnerability; some experience—like old age—where you opt for living or life destroys you. Your pattern of life is interrupted. You learn to be still, alert, so that the real is recognizable. You know yourself, not some statistic. You know not a theology of God, but the much more mysterious God of theology, the God of Abraham and Moses, of Isaiah and Ezekiel, the God of Peter, Paul, and John, the God of saints and the God of sinners.

A second suggestion: develop a feeling for festivity. Festivity, Josef Pieper insists, resides in activity that is meaningful in itself. I mean activity that is not tied to other goals, not tied to "so that" and "in order to." Festivity, therefore, calls for renunciation: you take usable time and withdraw it from utility. And this you do out of love, whose expression is joy. Festivity is essential to ideal aging, because festivity is a yes to the world, a yes to the reality of things, a yes to the existence of man and woman; it is a yes to the world's Creator.

A third suggestion, intimately allied to festivity: don't try to "possess" the object of your delight, whether God or man, imprisoned marble or free-flowing rivulet; and don't expect to "profit" from contemplation, from pleasure. Here Kerr's *Decline of Pleasure* has a profound paragraph that has powerfully affected my life:

> To regain some delight in ourselves and in our world, we are forced to abandon, or rather to reverse, an adage. A bird in the hand is *not* worth two in the bush—unless one is an ornithologist, the curator of the Museum of Natural History, or one of those Italian vendors who supply restaurants with larks. A bird in the hand is no longer a bird at all: it is a specimen; it may be dinner. Birds are birds only when they are in the bush or on the wing; their worth as birds can only be known at a discreet and generous distance.

A fourth suggestion: read, make friends with, remarkable men and women who have themselves looked long and lovingly at the real. I mean Augustine of Hippo and Antoine de Saint Exupéry, Catherine of Siena and Margaret Mead, Nikos Kazantzakis and Lao-Tzu, Julian of Norwich and Anne Morrow Lindbergh, Teresa of Avila and John of the Cross, Dag Hammarskjöld and Dr. Zhivago, Thomas Merton and Thomas More, Gandhi and Thoreau, Dietrich Bonhoeffer and Abraham Joshua Heschel, and a host of others. But note what kind of men and women these are: not solitaries, not hermits, not neurotic escapists, but flesh and blood in a flesh-and-blood world, unique however because each of them struggled daringly for self-transcendence, each smashed through boundaries and stretched humankind's limits to the walls of infinity.

Have I gotten away from the aging? Quite the contrary. As I see it, all our agonizing efforts to make aging palatable will be band-aid remedies unless the elderly can move through kenosis to contemplation. The task is awesome indeed; for that task is to create a new climate—social and economic, political and psychological—where the aging can be freed to look long and lovingly at the real, freed to see themselves and their world as these really are, freed to grow inside by growing in oneness with God and with all that God has so lavishly fashioned, to laugh once again because so much of human activity is absurdly incongruous, to rejoice and be glad because *this* day of their lives the Lord has made!

THEY WINTERED GRACEFULLY

Fortunately for our realistic hoping, there *are* people who age that way. From my vocation to Jesuit existence, I prize, perhaps inevitably, certain of my colleagues who grew old gracefully. I choose from among many John LaFarge, Teilhard de Chardin, and Horace McKenna.

Member of a distinguished family of artists and authors, John LaFarge (1880–1963) labored for fifteen years in the rural missions of southern Maryland and founded the Catholic interracial movement in the U.S. Wonderfully wide-ranging, he was active in liturgical arts, international peace, and rural life, was honored by Jews and Catholics, feted by scholars, loved by the deprived. On turning seventy, Uncle John (as his colleagues on the weekly *America* fondly styled him) wrote a moving article to show how faith can transform old age, if one has a definite purpose and program. The program? Old age is a time of prayer, a time of charity, and a time for courage.

A time of prayer. Not monastic isolation, only a deepening of value. Greater familiarity with God and His saints; prayer now a part of life's texture; the familiar (Mass, the *De profundis*) taking on fresh meaning. Listening for the Voice once drowned out by younger clamorings, now clearly heard in the cool of evening. More consciously grateful for the years behind, for the present moment; each day is a gift. Prayer less private, absorbed into "the great sacramental intercession of the Mystical Body of Christ."

A time of charity. The area of operation has narrowed, of course. A kind word, a quiet service; visiting the lonely and listening to the young; sharing the sadness of the bereaved, the gladness of the newly wed; encouraging creative effort; charity for those spiritually kin to us but separated by misunderstanding or honest differences or even prejudice. Love for the living and love for the dead.

A time for courage. Indeed a time for precautions—from the railing on the stairs to the coat over chilled shoulders to the salt-free diet. And yet, the very "fact that so little of life still remains is the added reason for being . . . prodigal of that little." Here is "when you place all your life, hopes and being in the hands of Him who gave His all for you." It's the courage to accept diminution—of adventure and achievement, of flesh and friends, of control, concentration, and communication. Welcoming diminution, going forth to meet it, embracing it. It can be "a vast liberation, not an imprisonment." It's the chance to rewrite our lives, perhaps the lives of others. With John LaFarge's faith, old age was summed up in the great offering of thanksgiving-reparation, the Mass: into this offering he set his own offering of life itself.

A sign of contradiction for twentieth-century Catholicism, Pierre Teilhard de Chardin (1881–1955) offered a seductive vision of the universe wherein matter and spirit, body and soul, nature and supernature, science and faith find their unity in Christ. Whatever one may think of his scientific methodology and the theological implications of his system, here was a priest-scholar of profound spirituality for whom the divine milieu is not only the mystical body of Christ but his cosmic body as well. "God is as out-stretched and tangible as the atmosphere in which we are bathed." Towards the close of his life he could write: "*Throughout* my life, *through* my life, the world has little by little caught fire in my sight until, aflame all around me, it has become almost completely luminous from within.... Such has been my experience in contact with the earth—the diaphany of the divine at the heart of the universe on fire.... Christ; his heart; a fire: capable of penetrating everywhere and, gradually, spreading everywhere."

Here was a man who, especially in *The Divine Milieu,* wrote with sensitivity and passion of our diminishments slow and swift—from our earliest defects, failings, and limitations, through a body rebellious and a personality in conflict, to "old age little by little robbing us of ourselves and pushing us on towards the end. Time, which postpones possession, time which tears us away from enjoyment, time which condemns us all to death—what a formidable passivity is the passage of time." In a moving prayer, Teilhard prayed to God for continuing communion through his very diminishing:

Now that I have found the joy of utilizing all forms of growth to make you, or to let you, grow in me, grant that I may willingly consent to this last phase of communion in the course of which I shall possess you by diminishing in you.

... When the signs of age begin to mark my body (and still more when they touch my mind); when the ill that is to diminish me or carry me off strikes from without or is born within me; when the painful moment comes in which I suddenly awaken to the fact that I am ill or growing old; and above all at that last moment when I feel I am losing hold of myself and am absolutely passive within the hands of the great unknown forces that have formed me; in all those dark moments, O God, grant that I may understand that it is you (provided only my faith is strong enough) who are painfully parting the fibres of my being in order to penetrate to the very marrow of my substance and bear me away within yourself....

You are the irresistible and vivifying force, O Lord, and because yours is the energy, because, of the two of us, you

are infinitely the stronger, it is on you that falls the part of
consuming me in the union that should weld us together.
Vouchsafe, therefore, something more precious still than the
grace for which all the faithful pray. It is not enough that I
should die while communicating. Teach me *to communicate
while dying.*

In May of '82 we buried a man of 83 in our nation's capital.
Few of the powerful knew Father Horace McKenna, for he
was one with the powerless. He simply lived Christ's criteria
for inheriting his kingdom (Mt 25:31–46). Were people
hungry? He founded SOME ("So Others Might Eat"), walked
there day after day to breakfast with the "street people"
SOME served. Were people strangers? For half a century he
labored to link black and white in love, gave blacks and poor
whites a sense of their dignity. Were people homeless? He inspired Sursum Corda ("Lift Up Your Hearts"), low-income
housing, placed families there, called each child by name; he
started the House of Ruth for homeless and abused women,
gave it its name and the first dollar for its property. Were people naked? He offered them showers and fresh clothing. Were
people sick? He visited them recklessly, however dangerous
the area. The first time I saw him in civies and tie (he was 75), I
expressed surprise: "Horace, what gives?" His response, with
that impish smile: "Some of the fathers at St. Al's kidded me
that I didn't have to worry about being mugged around there,
because I always wore the Roman collar; so I thought I'd see
what it would be like without the collar."

Horace McKenna described himself as a man with a stole
and an apron—the twin symbols of his service. Like his Lord,
he could grow black with anger, but only if *others* were hurt-
ing. At countless speeches his head slumped to his chest early;
but at the end it invariably popped up with the same old question: "And what of the poor?" And yet he was never narrow.
He encouraged us crusty eggheads who are poor only in spirit,

and he always had time for the fledglings at Gonzaga High, even for their *West Side Story* when he could no longer see the players. No man, woman, or child ever bored him; for, as he said on his deathbed in the Georgetown University Hospital, one lesson above all others he had learned in living: "the presence of Jesus Christ in every human being." No wonder that when Horace McKenna died, Southern Maryland and Washington wept.

Horace McKenna's achievements were amazing indeed. Even more amazing was how, through life's last diminishments, life still delighted him, people of all ages still turned him on, injustice still angered him and love left him aglow. Almost blind, he could still "see" you with startling insight; led about by others' hands, he never stopped moving out to the other. It was more than human—and possible only because he had always submerged his weakness in another's strength: "I have been crucified with Christ; it is no longer I who live, but Christ who lives in me; and the life I now live in the flesh I live by faith in the Son of God, who loved me and gave himself for me" (Gal 2:20).

It would be graceless to leave the impression that graceful aging is a Jesuit preserve. Recently I read a moving account of the cellist Pablo Casals. At ninety he was dreadfully afflicted by rheumatoid arthritis and emphysema. Each new day was agony. He could hardly dress himself. He would shuffle into the living room each morning on the arm of his lovely young wife Marta, badly stooped, head pitched forward. He would move to the piano, arrange himself with difficulty on the bench, somehow raise his swollen, clenched fingers above the keyboard. Let Norman Cousins, long-time distinguished editor of the *Saturday Review,* tell you what he saw:

> I was not prepared for the miracle that was about to happen. The fingers slowly unlocked and reached toward the keys

like the buds of a plant toward the sunlight. His back
straightened. He seemed to breathe more freely. Now his
fingers settled on the keys. Then came the opening bars of
Bach's [*Well-tempered Clavichord*], played with great sensitivity and control.... He hummed as he played, then said
that Bach spoke to him here—and he placed his hand over
his heart.

Then he plunged into a Brahms concerto and his fingers,
now agile and powerful, raced across the keyboard with daz-
zling speed. His entire body seemed fused with the music; it
was no longer stiff and shrunken but supple and graceful and
completely freed of its arthritic coils.

Having finished the piece, he stood up by himself, far
straighter and taller than when he had come into the room.
He walked to the breakfast table with no trace of a shuffle,
ate heartily, talked animatedly, finished the meal, then went
for a walk on the beach.

Such grace-full aging I found powerfully symbolized several years ago. A fellow Jesuit and former colleague at Georgetown, Eugene Geinzer, is a sculptor of uncommon creativity.
One product of his art, entitled "Vulnerability," is a bed made
of hard, uncompromising wood. Visually, it does not seem able
to ease the body into sleep. Yet it yields to the convexities of
the body; it is carved to receive the body.

This bed is equipped with pillories at head and foot.
Worse still, the pillories are adjustable to stretch to the limits of
the body. We seem to be looking at a rack. Neither head nor
chest nor trunk nor groin is protected. The limbs which might
otherwise defend the body are stretched out defenseless.

But this is the superficial story. When you lie down on this
bed, it is carved to hold your body gently. It is not hostile to
your shape; it accommodates itself. It is not a Procrustean bed.
Even the pillories reveal themselves not as mechanisms of torture but something to stretch yourself upon easily, the way a
cat or balletist might. If anything, it feels like an exercising

board. What you seem to see is challenged by what you feel. On this bed you can actually relax your muscles, be invigorated. What seems designed to torture you is really a way of setting you at peace.

This is, as you might suspect, a repercussion of the ambiguous character of our personal cross, of pain. What we discover in our vulnerability is that what threatens us with destruction can, if eased into, give our body and our spirit their rest.

SUFFERING

To speak of vulnerability is to raise the issue of suffering. Not that suffering afflicts the aging alone. Little children suffer from Tay-Sachs disease and starve on refugee roads; young executives are stricken by strokes, and the life expectancy for men and women in Bangladesh is 35.8; the middle-aged feel the finiteness in their flesh, increasingly seek the analyst's couch, at times find refuge in alcohol or death. But it is the old who bear life's burdens precisely because of their age, bear them day after day, bear them with little or no hope from the dominant culture.

Frankly, I have found no "explanation" of suffering that satisfies the mind. Suffering enmeshes us in the problem of evil, and despite all the efforts of the philosophers evil remains very much a mystery. The Old Testament traces suffering to sin—the sin of parents, the sin of the nation, one's own sin; it sees in suffering a test of virtue, of fidelity to God; suffering enables the victim to atone for others. Yet even here there is no "answer." Remember how Job wrestled with God? In the face of evil—the innocent suffering, the wicked prospering—he found human wisdom bankrupt. His anguished questioning ended in a theophany: God appeared to him, not to defend His wisdom but to stress His mystery. Job trusted God not because he could prove that God merited his trust, but because he had experienced God. Ultimately, he trusted God because he loved Him. God had shown Job His face.

In the Christian vision the mystery does not disappear, it is simply enriched. It is through suffering, for us and in our stead, that God-in-flesh destroyed the power of sin and death; and it is through suffering that we "complete in [our] flesh what is lacking in Christ's afflictions for the sake of his body, that is, the Church" (Col 1:24). But as with Job, so with me: I cannot prove that my pain is redemptive; suffering will only make sense if Christ has shown his face to me.

I sense this sort of experience in that tough yet gentle woman Rose Fitzgerald Kennedy, now 92. Her life has been darkened by tragedy: the assassination of sons Jack and Bobby; the death of Joe Jr. in war; daughter Kathleen killed in a plane crash, daughter Rosemary retarded. . . . What enables her to sparkle and laugh, to love every moment of life, swim before lunch, stay interested in books and politics, genuinely enjoy 29 grandchildren and four great-grandchildren? Basically, a profound faith, hope, and love: "It's the religious feeling that God is all-good and that He won't give us any cross that is impossible for us to bear, that I've had so many great favors given to me by everyone and everywhere, that I should be strong myself and help other people rather than depending on them to help me." Books and articles "expose" a ruthless, romancing husband; yet she never had an argument with him through 55 years. "I married for love and I got plenty of it." Rose Kennedy's cane is not a crutch. It's a way of reaching out to others: to God in daily Mass, to the deprived and underprivileged in daily giving. No self-pity; only gratitude for the gift of life.

A Christian like Rose Kennedy doesn't look for a theology of suffering, an explanation of evil. Suffering is simply there, to be lived with, to be lived. But not stoically, resignedly, stiff upper lip—"mustn't let on, you know." The difference is a person: Christ. Christ who lives in her. Christ dying and rising. It is his dying and rising that the faith-full Christian reproduces day after day. This is the way it has to be; for if the dying and rising of Jesus is not the constant rhythm of my life, I am less than Christian. And so I often wish that, instead of looking for a profound explanation of evil, I could simply immerse myself in the mystery of Christ, where love transmutes sheer suffering into redemptive sacrifice. I wish that at the Eucharistic consecration I were more clearly murmuring "This is *my* body, which is given up for you." There is so much to learn about suffering if we can only put our reasoning to rest awhile, if like the disciple "whom Jesus loved" we would only lie "close to the breast of Jesus" (Jn 13:23).

This is the kind of lived theology you find in people like Dr. Tom Dooley, who gave his hands and his heart to the poor in Laos, originated a program (MEDICO) to bring mercy medicine to backward areas the world over, and at 34 died of malignant melanoma—"a gift" he called it, a gift from God, a gift to be used. "I knew I was not going to abandon what I think is the correct thing to do in life because of shadows on a page. Nor was I going to quit this living, loving passion for life that I possess simply because of a statistic [the pessimistic statistics on survival in melanoma]. I was not abandoning the beauty and tenderness that man can give to man, just for a statistic."

If Tom Dooley could say this in the summer of life, I should be able to say it in life's winter. Suffering is a gift. Not a good thing in itself; in itself it is the absence of something good. But good if it is my yes to the redemptive work of Christ, my yes to Gethsemani and Calvary. Not a naked syllable supinely affirming his passion; rather, the insertion of my life into his. Yes, my life: each moment, each twinge of the flesh as well as each rapture of the heart. For Christianity is not, in the first instance, a set of regulations and obligations I must observe if I am to reach heaven. Christianity is a way of life in which (to use the traditional Morning Offering) "my prayers, works, joys, and sufferings of this day" continue through time what Christ began but could not finish "in the days of his flesh" (Heb 5:7).

The theology is clear enough, but how do you come to live it? Only, I suggest, through close intimacy with Christ. This I saw in the living *Pietà* of my mother cradling the lifeless bodies of my father and brother, dead within three weeks of each other. Until her memory deserted her a quarter century later, she lived the agony of a husband and a son wasting away on hospital beds. And still she lived—this seemingly frail woman who shoveled 25 tons of coal to heat the flats she janitored for several months after my father died, this sensitive woman who must have been unbearably lonely and yet was a ceaseless source of strength to the heavy-burdened. She simply lived, lived simply, in God's presence. God was real to her—the abiding experience of Another that shaped her, roughly and rudely at times, to the dying-rising Christ.

DEATH

All well and good—so far. But even if my oneness with Christ lends a Christian sense to suffering, even if I achieve through contemplation a measure of integration that wards off despair, I must still face the ultimate in *dis*integration. I mean . . . death.

How come to terms with death? Skeptic that I am, I doubt that most Christians yearn, with St. Paul, "to depart and to be with Christ" (Phil 1:23). Most pass early through Kübler-Ross's first four stages of the actually dying: I deny death's imminence; I get angry at death; I bargain; I am depressed. Why? I will not admit, as some charge, that my fear of death is basically my fear of life. I cannot resonate to those who view death as part of a movement naturally upward and positive—like the butterfly leaving the cocoon, like the fetus breaking the amnion. I feel at times much closer to the respected medical doctor who wrote in a respected medical journal: "death is an insult; the stupidest, ugliest thing that can happen to a human being."

Why an insult? Because in death a unique I, an irreplaceable thou, is destroyed. I who lift my eyes to the stars and only yesterday looked down on snow-capped Alps ... I who catch with my ears the rapture of Ravel's *Boléro* and once throbbed to the music of my mother's voice ... I who breathe the smog of our nation's capital, whose nostrils twitch to the odor of Veal Scaloppine ... I who cradle the Christ in my hands and whose lips thrill to a kiss ... I who run my fingers lazily through water and gently caress the face of a friend ... I whose mind ranges over centuries and continents, to share Plato's world of ideas and Gandhi's passion for peace ... I who laugh and love, worry and weep, dance and dream, sing and sin, preach and pray— this I will be lost to the world, this thou lost to those who survive me.

There is a darkness to death which even the Son of God cried out against. Death has a blank face; death is cruel; death breaks the whole person; I, I, I will vanish from living reach and touch. And so I fear that, like Dylan Thomas, I shall "not go gentle into that good night." I am much more likely to "burn and rave at close of day;/ Rage, rage against the dying of the light."

Aware of death's darkness, I find I need a fresh conversion to the risen Christ. What was once credal affirmation, "we look for the resurrection of the dead," becomes literally life or death. I am disturbed by Christian theologians who insist that personal survival doesn't matter all that much. I cry with Paul: "If Christ has not been raised, then [my] preaching is in vain and [my] faith is in vain. . . . [I am] still in [my] sins. . . . If for this life only we have hoped in Christ, we are of all men and women most to be pitied" (1 Cor 15:14, 17, 19). If heaven is not for real, I shall be madder than hell.

There are indeed moments when the *idea* of a God who transcends time and space and yet cares for me seems absurd, when "the grace of the Lord Jesus Christ and the love of God and the fellowship of the Holy Spirit" (2 Cor 13:14) sounds unreal, when the risen body is less believable than the strange, lovable creature E.T. in Steven Spielberg's movie. There are times when I am driven to my knees to pray "I believe, Lord; help my unbelief." But on the whole, there is the joy Jesus promised, the joy no man or woman (save ourselves) can take from us, the joy summed up in six short words: "I live, and you shall live" (Jn 14:19). In my most Christian moments I expect that the Spirit who never ceases to surprise me—with sorrow and joy, through events and people—will surprise me singularly at the moment I die.

I cannot begin to imagine what it will be like (bestriding clouds and gazing on God for eternity fail to turn me on). I know only that it will be an experience of God without parallel this side of death, that the experience will satisfy my deepest needs and longings. I believe, against all the evidence, that the Lord Jesus "will change our lowly body to be like his glorious body" (Phil 3:21), that my ultimate integration will be one whole person in the image of the risen Christ, whole because utterly free of St. Paul's fourfold slavery: enslavement to sin and death, to law and self.

Death as freedom. A startling thought. It recalls that astonishing Lutheran pastor Dietrich Bonhoeffer, who at 39 was hanged in the concentration camp at Flossenbürg because he had conspired to overthrow Hitler.

Here was a German who returned to Germany from New York in 1939 because he felt he would have no right to help reconstruct Christian life in postwar Germany if he did not share the wartime anguish of his people. A Christian who agonized over Christian complicity with Hitler on war and the Jews. A churchman who could no longer endure the Church's silence when the blood of the innocent was crying to heaven. An ethicist who came to believe that in extraordinary situations there is no law behind which the responsible man or woman can seek cover—only a complete renunciation of every law. A theologian who wrote from prison that only by living unreservedly in the bittersweet of this life can one become human and Christian. A prisoner who even gave thought to suicide, not because he felt guilty but because basically he was already dead. A disciple who experienced to the full what he had called so poignantly "the cost of discipleship."

Bonhoeffer's grasp on freedom as our imaging of God (free *for* the other, free *from* the creature, be that creature a suffocating technology, a tyrannical Führer, or an enslaved church) was climaxed in the prison days after the July 20, 1944 attempt to assassinate Hitler failed—climaxed in the remarkable prison poem "Stations on the Road to Freedom":

Discipline

If you set out to seek freedom, then learn above all things
to govern your soul and your senses, for fear that your passions
and longing[s] may lead you away from the path you should follow.
Chaste be your mind and your body, and both in subjection,
obediently, steadfastly seeking the aim set before them;
only through discipline may a man learn to be free.

Action

Daring to do what is right, not what fancy may tell you,
valiantly grasping occasions, not cravenly doubting—
freedom comes only through deeds, not through thoughts taking
    wing.
Faint not nor fear, but go out to the storm and the action,
trusting in God whose commandment you faithfully follow;
freedom, exultant, will welcome your spirit with joy.

Suffering

A change has come indeed. Your hands, so strong and active,
are bound; in helplessness now you see your action
is ended; you sigh in relief, your cause committing
to stronger hands; so now you may rest contented.
Only for one blissful moment could you draw near to touch
    freedom;
then, that it might be perfected in glory, you gave it to God.

Death

Come now, thou greatest of feasts on the journey to freedom
    eternal;
death, cast aside all the burdensome chains, and demolish
the walls of our temporal body, the walls of our souls that are
    blinded,
so that at last we may see that which here remains hidden.
Freedom, how long we have sought thee in discipline, action, and
    suffering;
dying, we now may behold thee revealed in the Lord.

Bonhoeffer's paean to death would be the sensible man's
dignified way of waving farewell to winter. For better or
worse, the author and editor in me cannot resist reproducing
the epitaph Benjamin Franklin presented to Samuel Morris in
Philadelphia on August 31, 1776:

> The Body of
> B. Franklin, Printer,
> Like the Cover of an old Book,
> Its Contents torn out,
> And stript of its Lettering and Gilding,
> Lies here, Food for Worms.
> But the Work shall not be lost,
> For it will, as he believ'd, appear once more
> In a new and more elegant Edition
> Corrected and improved
> By the Author.

So be it. . . .

POSTLUDE

As I compose these final measures, my Sound of Music is not "16 going on 17"; it is 68 going on 69. The stark numbers are at times dismaying; and still the feeling that suffuses me these days is quite other. I would call it . . . joy in living.

It is not that my head is in clouds. In the Prelude, you may remember, I spoke of memories that are dangerous, because they make demands on us, reveal perilous insights for today, illuminate harshly the questionable nature of things with which we have come to terms. Many such memories haunt me, are in fact present realities. I am thinking of a Holocaust that most Americans would just as soon forget; the world-wide threat to life in war and womb, through hunger and injustice; the undignified "graying of America," the indignity in growing old; the 12 million without work, especially minorities; the cold war between black and white, between the have's and the have-not's; children battered, bruised, and burned; women treated as second-class citizens; polarization in the Catholic community; the inability of 50% of married men and women to say "forever"; the resurgence of rugged individualism, with "I" at the center of existence; prisons without hope; refugees clogging the world's roads and its camps; the trivialization of sex; the burgeoning principle that if I enjoy it and it doesn't hurt anyone, it must be right and good.

And still I am glad and rejoice. I joy more than ever in my work—research and writing, lecturing and preaching, editing and counseling. In so much of this I resonate to the experience of the virtuoso Claudio Arrau after 65 years at the piano: "Now I play with more joy and abandon and confidence and discipline than I ever have before."

I joy in people—beyond counting. In my brothers in the Society of Jesus; for despite the pettiness that can stalk unisex existence, I find here a community of openness, a community of acceptance, a community that supports me without strangling me, a community on which I depend without being enslaved to it. In friends who never cease to inspire me with their courage and faith, delight me with their warmth and wit, keep me reasonably sane with their practical wisdom. In so many students at Georgetown who are my link to youthful vitality, my tie to the forces of growth in myself and in the world, the forces that keep me creative.

I joy, above all, in a gift beyond compare, a gift poignantly expressed by a remarkable rabbi. Several years before his death in 1972, Abraham Joshua Heschel suffered a near-fatal heart attack from which he never fully recovered. A dear friend visiting him then found him woefully weak. Just about able to whisper, Heschel said to him: "Sam, when I regained consciousness, my first feeling was not of despair or anger. I felt only gratitude to God for my life, for every moment I had lived. I was ready to depart. 'Take me, O Lord,' I thought, 'I have seen so many miracles in my lifetime.' " Exhausted by the effort, Heschel paused, then added: "That is what I meant when I wrote [in the preface to his book of Yiddish poems]: 'I did not ask for success; I asked for wonder. And You gave it to me.' "

ACKNOWLEDGEMENTS

(in order of appearance)

PRELUDE: Henri Nouwen, *The Living Reminder* (Seabury, 1977) 25

Daniel J. Levinson, *The Seasons of a Man's Life* (Knopf, 1978) used as a framework throughout

Richard Bach, *Illusions: The Adventures of a Reluctant Messiah* (Dell/Eleanor Friede, 1977) [4], 190–91, 192

SPRING: *The Simone Weil Reader* (David McKay, c1977) 12

Paul Elmem, "Death of an Elfking," *Christian Century* 94, no. 37 (Nov. 16, 1977) 1057, quotation from Robert Lowell

François Truffaut, *The 400 Blows,* in *The Adventures of Antoine Doinel: Four Screenplays by François Truffaut* (Simon and Schuster, c1971) passim

The Short Novels of John Steinbeck (Viking, 1953) passim from *The Red Pony* and a sentence from Joseph Henry Jackson's Introduction

Erik Erikson, *Insight and Responsibility* (Norton, c1964) 125

Ernest Hemingway, *The Old Man and the Sea* (Scribner's, 1952) 10, 12, 17, 18, 25, 138

Piet Smulders, *The Design of Teilhard de Chardin* (Newman, 1967) 176–77

St. Augustine, *Confessions* 2, 2–4 passim, from the translation by F. J. Sheed, *The Confessions of St. Augustine* (Sheed & Ward, 1943) 27–32

Mary McCarthy, *Memories of a Catholic Girlhood* (Harcourt, Brace & World, 1946) 21

Joseph Plunkett, "I See His Blood upon the Rose," *The Oxford Book of Irish Verse: XVIIth Century—XXth Century* (Clarendon, 1958) 208

Time, Nov. 12, 1979, 42, on Cambodian refugees

Andrew Greeley, "A Post-Vatican II New Breed?" *America* 142, no. 25 (June 28, 1980) 537

James J. DiGiacomo, "Teaching the Next New Breed," *America* 144, no. 25 (June 27, 1981) 518–22

Arthur Simon, *Bread for the World* (Paulist, 1975) 14

Time, Sept. 1, 1980, 56, data on teen-age suicides

Daniel Offer, Eric Ostrov, and Kenneth I. Howard, *The Adolescent: A Psychological Self-Portrait* (Basic Books, 1981) data summarized

Torey L. Hayden, *One Child* (Avon, c1980) 10, 64, 70, 90, 104, 138, 185, 201, 205, 206, 220–21

SUMMER: John Courtney Murray, S.J., "The Danger of the Vows," *Woodstock Letters* 96 (1967) 421–27

Carin Rubinstein, "Money & Self-Esteem, Relationships, Secrecy, Envy, Satisfaction," *Psychology Today* 15, no. 5 (May 1981) 29–44, esp. 40–44

Philip Rieff, *Freud: The Mind of the Moralist* (Doubleday Anchor Books, 1961) 65, 361–62, 390, 391

George Herbert, "Love (III)," in *The Works of George Herbert,* ed. F. E. Hutchinson (Clarendon, 1941) 188–89

Simone Weil, "Spiritual Autobiography," in *The Simone Weil Reader* (David McKay, c1977) 16, 18, 21, 23

St. Augustine, *Confessions* 2, 1; 3, 1; 6, 15; 8, 7; 8, 8; 8, 12, from the translation by Sheed, *op. cit.* 27, 41, 126, 170, 171, 178–79

John Gruen, "The Saint—An Opera That Mirrors Menotti's Soul," *New York Times,* Sunday, April 16, 1978, "Arts and Leisure" 19

Elie Wiesel, *The Gates of the Forest* (Reinhart and Winston, c1966) 194

John Pick, ed., *A Hopkins Reader* (Oxford University Press, 1953) xii

The Journals and Papers of Gerard Manley Hopkins, ed. Humphry House (Oxford University Press, 1959) 71, 165

The Correspondence of Gerard Manley Hopkins and Richard Watson Dixon, ed. Claude Colleer Abbott (2nd [rev.] impression; Oxford University Press, 1955) 14, 15

Further Letters of Gerard Manley Hopkins, ed. Claude Colleer Abbott (2nd ed. rev.; Oxford University Press, 1956) 231

The Poems of Gerard Manley Hopkins, ed. W. H. Gardner and N. H. MacKenzie (4th ed.; Oxford University Press, 1970) 31, 60, 66, 87, 98

Pius X, Encyclical *Vehementer nos,* Feb. 11, 1906 (*ASS* 39 [1906] 8–9)

Ashley Montagu, *The Elephant Man: A Study in Human Dignity* (Dutton, 1979) 14–16, 18, 22, 29, 34, 63–64, 77

Flannery O'Connor: The Habit of Being. Letters edited by Sally Fitzgerald (Farrar, Straus, Giroux, c1979) xvi, 57, 90, 92, 124, 125, 126, 221, 258, 266, 307–8, 310, 348, 354, 407, 419, 430, 453, 509, 527, 572

AUTUMN: John W. O'Malley, S.J., "Reform, Historical Consciousness, and Vatican II's Aggiornamento," *Theological Studies* 32 (1971) 600

Carl R. Rogers, *On Becoming a Person: A Therapist's View of Psychotherapy* (Houghton Mifflin, c1961) 26

Henri J. M. Nouwen, *The Wounded Healer: Ministry in Contemporary Society* (Doubleday, 1972) 74

Monica Furlong, *Merton: A Biography* (Harper & Row, c1980) esp. 202–340 passim

John Eudes Bamberger, "In Search of Thomas Merton," *America* 147, no. 9 (Oct. 2, 1982) 165–69

Andrew M. Greeley, *The Mary Myth: On the Femininity of God* (Seabury, 1977) 145

Time, March 3, 1980, 66, and Aug. 4, 1980, 61, on Peter Sellers

Where Have I Been? Sid Caesar. An Autobiography with Bill Davidson (Crown, c1982) passim

Monika Hellwig, "Transforming Power of the Eucharist," *National Bulletin on Liturgy* 15, no. 82 (Jan.–Feb. 1982) 43

William F. Lynch, S.J., "The Catholic Idea," in *The Idea of Catholicism: An Introduction to the Thought and Worship of the Church,* ed. Walter J. Burghardt, S.J., and William F. Lynch, S.J. (Meridian Books, 1960) 60–61

Henri de Lubac, S.J., "Meditation on the Church," in *Vatican II: An Interfaith Appraisal,* ed. John H. Miller, C.S.C. (University of Notre Dame, c1966) 259–60, 261

WINTER: Simone de Beauvoir, *The Coming of Age* (Warner, 1973) 322–23

Walter Kerr, *The Decline of Pleasure* (Simon and Schuster, 1962) 210–11, 245

John LaFarge, "On Turning Seventy," *America* 106, no. 7 (Nov. 16, 1961) 242–45

Pierre Teilhard de Chardin, *The Divine Milieu: An Essay on the Interior Life* (Harper, c1960) 14, 54, 62–63

Norman Cousins, *Anatomy of an Illness as Perceived by the Patient: Reflections on Healing and Regeneration* (Bantam Books, 1981) 72–73

George Esper, "Rose at 92: A House of Love and Laughter," *Washington Times,* July 21, 1982, 1B-2B

Agnes W. Dooley, *Promises to Keep: The Life of Doctor Thomas A. Dooley* (New American Library, 1964) 153–54

The Collected Poems of Dylan Thomas (New Directions, 1971) 128

Dietrich Bonhoeffer, *Letters and Papers from Prison,* enlarged ed. by Eberhard Bethge (SCM, 1971) 37–71

POSTLUDE: Samuel H. Dresner, "Remembering Abraham Heschel," *America* 146, no. 21 (May 29, 1982) 414